The aim of the Biblical Classics Library is to make
available at the lowest prices new editions of
classic titles by well-known scholars. There is
a particular emphasis on making these books
affordable to Eastern Europe and the
Two-Thirds World.

For current listing see overleaf

Once Saved,
Always Saved

D1321899

Authors in the Biblical Classics Library:

C.K. Barrett
   The Signs of an Apostle (19)
F.F. Bruce
   Men and Movements in the Primitive Church (13)
   The Message of the New Testament (1)
   The Pauline Circle (14)
David Burnett
   The Healing of the Nations (18)
D.A. Carson
   From Triumphalism to Maturity (20)
   Jesus and His Friends (15)
   The Sermon on the Mount (2)
   When Jesus Confronts the World (16)
H.L. Ellison
   Men Spake from God (9)
   The Message of the Old Testament (3)
John Goldingay
   God's Prophet, God's Servant (5)
Graeme Goldsworthy
   Gospel and Kingdom (4)
   Gospel and Wisdom (10)
   The Gospel in Revelation (6)
J.H. Greenlee
   Scribes, Scrolls and Scripture (17)
A.M. Hunter
   Introducing New Testament Theology (26)
R.T. Kendall
   Believing God (11)
   Does Jesus Care? (25)
   Jonah (12)
   Once Saved, Always Saved (28)
I. Howard Marshall
   The Work of Christ (7)
Leon Morris
   The Cross of Jesus (8)
J.N. Schofield
   Introducing Old Testament Theology (27)
Thomas Smail
   The Forgotten Father (23)
Helmut Thielicke
   A Little Exercise for Young Theologians (24)
John Wenham
   Easter Enigma (22)
A.M. Wolters
   Creation Regained (21)

Once Saved, Always Saved

R.T. KENDALL

paternoster
press

First published in the UK 1983
by Ambassador Productions Ltd., Providence House,
16 Hillview Avenue, Belfast

This edition published 1997 by
Paternoster Press in the Biblical Classics Library

03 02 01 00 99 98 97   7 6 5 4 3 2 1

Paternoster Press in an imprint of Paternoster Publishing,
P.O. Box 300, Carlisle, Cumbria CA3 0QS

British Library Cataloguing in Publication Data

A catalogue record for this book is available from the British Library.

ISBN 0–85364–796–8

Printed in Great Britain by Mackays of Chatham PLC, Kent

Contents

Preface

I was not prepared for the shock waves this book sent after its first printing nine years ago. On the positive side, I have received countless testimonies from various parts of the world that this book has given people assurance of salvation for the first time in their lives and motivated them more than ever to holy living. This is precisely what I wanted and it is why I wrote the book. But on the other hand, I have found myself embroiled in controversy as a result of some reaction in certain quarters wherein I was accused of the very thing I sought to oppose - antinomianism: the dangerous teaching that, since we are eternally saved, how we live does not matter.

The issue is simple: if we are assured by our good works, we are within a hair's breadth of salvation by works. But what I have sought to show, and wherein my contribution chiefly lies, is that the charge of antinomianism is nullified by the New Testament teaching on the Kingdom of God, chastening and the Judgment Seat of Christ. And yet much of what I have taught has been said before by wiser and greater men than me.

What is wrong with the teaching that, though we are saved by Christ's death, we are assured of its benefit by our own works? Because it brings no assurance after all. It is 'safe' teaching - that is, invulnerable to the charge of antinomianism, but, it never delivers the goods. Who can say for sure he is absolutely certain of his salvation because his good works are good enough? He will always be in doubt. The inevitable result: legalism, bondage and fear.

I have had countless discussions with friends and 'foes' on this matter. At the end of the day one has got to come down on one side or the other: to be vulnerable to the charge of legalism or vulnerable to the charge of antinomianism.

I hope I will be forgiven for quoting Dr. Martyn Lloyd-Jones, a former minister of Westminster Chapel, on this issue. I say that because one must be prepared to stand on his own two feet and not take refuge in such respected territory as inhabited by the late Doctor. But he used to say to me again and again that if our preaching is not accused of being antinomian it is because we haven't really preached the gospel!

One reformed reviewer curiously wrote that what I have taught in *Once Saved, Always Saved* is true but that I shouldn't say it! This is because he thinks that a holy living is better generated by one having fear that he or she just may not be saved!

Wrong. Holy living that is not motivated by New Testament principles is phoney. This book is aimed to set one free from bondage but stir one to godly fear as the Judgment Seat of Christ obviously did for the Apostle Paul.

I turned down the opportunity to re-write this book or change parts of it for a new edition. I stand by what I have written. I might indeed make some sentences slightly clearer and I could elaborate on and on but then I could be protesting too much! All that is new in the present edition is an appendix that did not appear in the original. What I do envisage in the near future is to write a book wholly devoted to the Judgment Seat of Christ as well as an exposition on Hebrews 6.

It is my prayer that the person of Jesus Christ and the freedom He gives will be more real to you. Not all of this book is simple. But I do believe that, despite certain theological terms and concepts, you will be rewarded if you press on to the end.

R.T. Kendall
London
May 1992

Introduction

I have not always believed in "once saved, always saved." Unlike tithing, which I was taught as far back as I can remember, the doctrine of eternal security was utterly alien to my own feelings and background. My church not only did not teach it, they despised it. It was labelled "damnable doctrine," "hellish teaching" and "dangerous." Those who believed it, mostly Baptists (it seemed at the time), were branded "eternal securitists" who carnally followed a theological position that was conceived by the devil. That my church often sang "Amazing grace! how sweet the sound!," written by an "eternal securitist" (if ever there was one) did not matter. I was taught that, though saved by trusting Jesus' death on the cross, I must remain faithful to Him or I would lose my salvation. Admittedly there were diverse views among the preachers I heard as to what fully constituted backsliding—the forfeiture of my salvation until I repented again—but there was never any doubt in my mind that, if I were to make it to heaven, it would be up to me. "God has done all He can do for you, now it is up to you."

Most Baptists I knew as a child only helped confirm this view of salvation with which I was spoonfed. Our next-door neighbours were Baptists. They never went to church. I had to go at least three times a week—"every time the door was opened," as my neighbours liked to describe our habit of church attendance. My friend (I'll call him Mick) would use my own basketball and my basketball court (in my backyard) with the other boys in the neighbourhood while I was carted off to the Wednesday night prayer meeting. Mick didn't ever go to church— even on Sunday night or Sunday morning! His parents smoked and drank heavily. The language they used could be heard a mile away and It was not the language of Zion. My father would often invite them to our church, especially if we were having a "revival," but they would not come along. I don't think that Mick was ever inside the door of my church.

But one day I was given a surprise invitation. Our next-door neighbour invited us to go to their church! The reason: to witness Mick's baptism the following Sunday night. I have never learned what led to Mick's decision to be baptised. But my parents allowed me to go to church with him. Although I was only twelve at the time (Mick was sixteen), I vividly remember the conversation we had on the way to his church, a local Baptist church in Kentucky. "I'll be glad when this is over," Mick said to me. "I've been trying to live straight for a week. I haven't even cursed. But after tonight I won't have to worry any more. After I get baptised I can live as I please. I can go back to the way I was before. But I will be saved." As best as I can recall, those were his exact words.

My parents' estimate of Baptists generally was not very flattering to the doctrine of eternal security. My grandmother was brought up in a Baptist church in Elliot County, Kentucky, where spittoons were placed between various pews for people to spit their tobacco juice during the worship! But my grandmother was delivered from all that and her views of Baptists didn't help their reputation in our household. The earmark of Baptist doctrine in my part of the world was the teaching of the unconditional eternal security of the believer. My parents were absolutely convinced that it was abominable teaching, if only by observing the lives of so many Baptists they knew. When I heard Mick say what he did on the night of his baptism, I was adequately confirmed in my parents' understanding of Baptists.

Whether my friend Mick was correctly reflecting the teaching of his pastor is for the moment beside the point. It is what he *thought* was true. And whether spiting chewing tobacco into a church spittoon was a very godly thing, or how often a person got drunk, did not matter. If a person was saved, he was saved. Once saved, always saved.

Given this background and introduction to Baptists generally and the doctrine of eternal security particularly it would hardly seem likely that one day I should write a book affirming "once saved, always saved." If I had a distinct advantage in writing a book on tithing because I was taught it by my father, I most certainly have had a disadvantage when it comes to the doctrine of the security of the believer.

I therefore approach this subject with my eyes wide open. I know something of the suspicions of people that are averse to this teaching. I know the Scriptures they use to disprove it. I know something about the examples they can use to substantiate their position. I could give them a lot more illustrations than they ever needed.

But I come to the reader with the conviction that the Bible teaches "once saved, always saved." I do not know where this expression originated or who was the first to put it in print. Perhaps someone will eventually let me know who said it first. I only believe that it is a phrase that is biblically and theologically sound. We are not saying once *baptised*, always saved. We are not saying once having made a *profession*, always saved. We are not saying once having *come forward* or *walked up an aisle*, always saved. It is once *saved*, always saved. A major portion of this book will have something to say about being *saved*.

It may be of interest to the reader to know something of how I came to change my own views. It was not from reading a book like this one. I sincerely doubt if it would have done any good in any case. As a matter of fact, I am not writing this to convince the person who does not believe this doctrine. I am writing to convince the person who wants to believe it but is afraid to believe it. As for those Christians who do not believe it, I have great sympathy for them. Nobody knows better than I where they are coming from and I totally understand their biases and fears. A book like this will hardly convince them for I do not think it would have convinced me. What convinced me was the Lord. I mean that literally, however pious or lofty it may sound. My coming to the views presented in this book is entirely the result of a spiritual experience I had a long time ago. It is an experience I can only conceive as being of the Lord.

The date was October 31, 1955. On a Monday morning, driving in my car from my pastorate in Palmer, Tennessee, on the way to attend classes at Trevecca Nazarene College in Nashville I had the near equivalent of a Damascus Road experience. I do not feel it would be wise to disclose all the details here. But what I can say is that about a quarter to eight that morning I felt a warm surging of the Spirit that came into my heart and that left my soul in a state of great rest and peace. It would not be an exaggeration to say that I was in ecstasy. The feeling lasted for days, even months. The person of Jesus was more real to me than my own existence—or anybody else's. The sense of the presence of God was beyond anything I had dreamed of. But that is not all. I knew I was eternally saved. Unconditionally saved. Saved. I knew it. No scripture in particular came to mind at the moment. I just knew I was saved forever *no matter what I ever did*. Not that it gave me a feeling of not caring what I did. Quite the contrary. I loved God and His word and His will more than ever. I just knew that I was eternally, unconditionally, and absolutely saved.

Word of this experience spread in the dormitory at Trevecca. I was a bit unwise in telling it to one or two close friends and the word spread all over the campus like wildfire. Rumours spread that I had received a "third work of grace." The reason for this will be obvious to readers who are aware of Wesleyan teaching. I had believed in two works of grace—regeneration (conversion) and sanctification (cleansing). "Then what happened to you?" my friends asked. "I don't know," I could only say. "I just know I am saved—eternally saved." "What do you mean eternally saved?" "I mean just that. I am eternally saved." One friend cautioned me. "John Wesley believed that for a while," he said, "but Wesley changed and so will you." I knew what he was trying to say to me. But somehow I *knew* I would not change in my new view. I knew I was eternally saved. Forever. It was, to put it mildly, a most wonderful feeling.

Perhaps the most important consequence of this experience was the way in which the holy Scriptures opened up to me. The Bible became a new book. I had a boldness and a fearlessness in reading the Bible. It became alive. I felt no need to be defensive as I read. I didn't care what I read or what it said. I just believed it. If I had any particular theological view that was wrong, I didn't mind having it cut right down. I didn't care what the result was. Let theological surgery be performed!

And what an operation it was. My theology was almost completely renovated. I saw things I sincerely believed were discovered entirely by me. I thought I was on to truth that nobody had seen since the apostle Paul. It is not the task of this book to go into all that I learned in the weeks and months that followed October 31, 1955. I am simply stating that it was this experience that convinced me of the truth of the unconditional security of the believer. Since then I have read many books on the subject. I have finished Trevecca College, completed seminary, and done research at Oxford. In the past twenty-seven years I have drawn two conclusions: first, I did not discover anything new after all; second, the doctrine of "once saved, always saved" is more biblically based than most of its own proponents have believed. Many who believe it are actually afraid of it. It is largely they who have watered it down. As an outsider, as it were, I propose to put in writing what I believe the Bible teaches on this subject. I do so for one reason: to encourage believers

1

Statement
Of The Doctrine

Before we proceed any further it is important that we
know exactly what we are talking about. What do we
mean, "once saved, always saved"? This chapter will of
necessity have to introduce certain theological terms.
But I will try to explain each term, however technical or
difficult it may sound at first. Every Christian is called
to be a Bible student. I therefore hope the reader will not
skip over this chapter because it may appear theological.

Before we introduce various terms let me give a
definition of the teaching we are affirming. *Whoever
once truly believes that Jesus was raised from the dead,
and confesses that Jesus is Lord, will go to heaven when
he dies*. But I will not stop there. *Such a person will go
to heaven when he dies no matter what work (or lack of
work) may accompany such faith.*

Some readers may have heard of the expression "the
perseverance of the saints." This phrase is taken from
some time-honoured confessions of faith. "They whom
God hath accepted in his Beloved, effectually called and
sanctified by his Spirit, can neither totally nor finally fall
away from the state of grace: but shall certainly perse-

vere therein to the end, and be eternally saved" (*Westminster Confession of Faith*, XIX:1, "Of the Perseverance of the Saints"). The *Philadelphia Confession of Faith* states the same doctrine in virtually the same words.

It has been thought by many of us that the doctrine of the security of the believer in some cases has gotten out of control in modern times. The point some would make is that historically the teaching was known as the "perseverance of the saints" not merely "once saved, always saved" (although affirming the truth of the latter phrase). What some therefore want to preserve is the idea that it is "perseverance" of "saints" that should be stressed, not the unconditional salvation of just anybody who claims to believe.

Let us be fair with this concern. Such people loathe the superficial type of Christianity that has become so common today. Such people want to preserve godliness within the context of saving faith (a phrase I will come back to). Take my childhood friend Mick. He had no intention whatever of amending his ways after his baptism. He wanted to "get it over with" so he could go back to his usual manner of life but still know nonetheless that he would go to heaven when he died.

For reasons like this there are those who want to uphold "perseverance of the saints" and are a bit uneasy with the phrase "eternal security" or even "once saved, always saved." Such people obviously feel that this is a distortion of the classical teaching of the perseverance of the saints.

But there is another way of looking at this. The way in which the classical doctrine of the perseverance of the saints is often upheld may also be a distortion of the biblical doctrine of the security of the believer. For if it is strictly "perseverance," or even "sainthood," that we are after in order to establish the biblical teaching, there is really no point in having the doctrine in the first place.

To put it another way, if only those who persevere in sainthood are saved, there would be hardly any objection to the teaching. If, for example, John Smith seems genuinely converted but lapses after a couple of years, it may be argued that he simply was not converted in the first place. On the other hand, if he is restored, it shows he may have been converted after all. But if he falls again, his conversion is in doubt again, and so on. Thus only the person who is living the godly life *at the time* of his death can be safely regarded as *saved*.

If that is what the Bible teaches, then faith gives very little purpose or comfort whatever. I would simply be back to the original view of my own background and assume that, though I am saved by trusting Jesus' death on the cross, I will have no *assuranc*e that I am saved unless I am also in a state of godly living at every moment. I will therefore not be deriving my comfort from Jesus' death (however much I may wish I could). I will be deriving my *real* comfort and assurance from my own works. Jesus' death may save me, but I cannot be too excited about that if I don't have good works to show that He has *really* saved me.

It seems to me, then, that a book is in order that offers an alternative to the idea of perseverance of saints but also to the sheer godless approach of my friend Mick (who, by the way, is today steeped in the Jehovah's Witnesses). If all we are doing is upholding the traditional doctrine of the perseverance of the saints, there is hardly a need for a book like this. Many books have been written that give an exposition of the old confessions.

But another point of clarification may be in order. I hope no one will take this as an attack upon the Westminster Confession. It is not that. I happen to love the Westminster Confession. My own country was born out of the basic theological conviction that lies behind the Westminster Confession. The Puritans that came to America are largely the ones who gave it her soul. I am grateful for this. I am grateful for my own parents, as a matter of fact. But if I must differ with them, it does not mean an attack upon them. They just *might* be wrong on a point or two.

The statement of doctrine in the second paragraph of this chapter is what this book is about. There is a sense in which all we have to say rises or falls with Romans 10:910: "That if thou shalt confess with thy mouth the Lord Jesus [Jesus is Lord, NIV], and shalt believe in thine heart that God hath raised him from the dead, thou shalt be saved. For with the heart man believeth unto righteousness; and with the mouth confession is made unto salvation.'

According to these verses two things are required in order to be "saved": first, believing in your heart that God raised Jesus from the dead; second, confessing Jesus as Lord. My definition of "once saved, always saved" may be divided into two headings.

Whoever once truly believes. The four words here give rise to four teachings, all of which are of immense importance. *Whoever*. This indicates what we may call the *free offer of the gospel*. The gospel is offered to every person. Jesus tasted death "for every man" (Hebrews 2:9). "For God so loved the world, that he gave his only begotten Son, that *whosoever* believeth in him should not perish, but have everlasting life" (John 3:16). "Whosoever will, let him take the water of life freely" (Revelation 22:17). If the free offer of the gospel is undermined in the slightest way, all else falls apart. It is of critical importance that the superstructure of the teaching "once saved, always saved" be laid upon the foundation of the free offer of the gospel. The gospel is for everybody because Christ died for all. It is because God so loved the "world" that a "whosoever" comes into play. On the other hand, whoever does not believe this gospel will *perish*. The assumption in John 3:16 is that the gospel is the only thing that can help a person. The assumption is that men will perish anyway. The only thing that can help is the gospel. But it is the "whosoever" who believes that is saved; he who does not is damned.

Once. Whoever *once* truly believes. I suppose that is the sore spot with so many. It is "once, not twice or three times or three hundred times. Once." One needs have only what John Calvin called the "least drop of faith." And one need have it but once. Why is this? It is not great faith that saves; it is faith in a great Saviour. One need only see the Sin Bearer once to be saved. For it is God who gives faith. As Charles Spurgeon used to put it, "There is life in a look." "And as Moses lifted up the serpent in the wilderness, even so must the Son of man be lifted up: that whosoever believeth in him should not perish, but have eternal life" (John 3:14-15). One can see from these two verses that *believing is seeing.* Here

23

Jesus alluded to the generation of Israel which was infested with poisonous snakes. Moses made a serpent of brass and put it on a pole, that "if a serpent had bitten any man, when he *beheld* the serpent of brass, he lived" (Numbers 21:9). "Every one which seeth the Son, and believeth on him, may have everlasting life: and I will raise him up at the last day" (John 6:40). Even if he sees the Son a thousand times, or a million times, he is no more saved than when he looked once. For the "once" sets God's promise into effectual operation.

Truly. Whoever once *truly* believes. Notice that John 6:40 says "seeth the Son, and believeth on him." Those snakebitten Israelites gazed at the serpent of brass *because* they believed Moses' word. Many saw Jesus. But not all believed on Him. It is the one who *looks* to Jesus because he believes His word that will be saved. Faith is not mere mental assent to a set of doctrines. It is not an uncritical acceptance of the teachings of the church (even if those teachings be correct). This is why Paul said, "If thou shalt confess with thy mouth the Lord Jesus, *and* shalt believe in thine *heart* that God hath raised him from the dead, thou shalt be saved" (Romans 10:9). One may superficially confess "Jesus is Lord" without anything having taken place in the *heart*. The crux of the matter is precisely here. If a person does not believe in his *heart* - "heart of hearts," as we might it put it today - he is not saved. It is being convinced. Persuaded. The Greek word for faith in the New Testament comes from a root word that essentially means "to persuade." Faith is persuasion.

Believes. Whoever once truly *believes*. Trusts. Nothing more, only trusting. It is not faith *plus* works, it is faith *without* works. "For by grace are ye saved through *faith*; and that not of yourselves: it is the gift of God: not of works, lest any man should boast" (Ephesians 2:8-9). "Therefore being justified by *faith*, we have peace with God through our Lord Jesus Christ" (Romans 5:1). "*Faith* was reckoned to Abraham for righteousness. How was it then reckoned? when he was in circumcision, or in un-circumcision? Not in circumcision, but in un-circumcision (Romans 4:9-10). That is why Paul could conclude that "a man is justified by *faith* without the deeds of the law" (Romans 3:28). When a person believes, then "his faith is counted for righteousness" (Romans 4:5). The righteousness that is required is answered by faith. Once faith is present, God "imputeth [puts to their credit] righteousness without works" (Romans 4:6). Such righteousness is in fact the righteousness of *God* (Romans 1:17) and it is too powerful to be rivaled by any subsequent work, good or bad. Therefore once a person truly believes, such faith is counted for a righteousness that cannot be undone. "For the wrath of man worketh not the righteousness of God" (James 1:20). As we shall see in more detail later, the doctrine of justification by faith alone is sufficient to demonstrate all that this book hopes to establish.

That Jesus was raised from the dead. I promised to return to the phrase "saving faith." It is an important phrase to grasp. Not all faith is saving, that is, not all faith secures one a home in heaven.

There are two essential ingredients that constitute saving faith: the proper *seat* of faith and the correct *object* of faith. We have already dealt with the seat of faith when we spoke of the *heart*. Saving faith is seated in the heart. Not the head (this is mental assent). Not even the desire. Both the head and the desire come into the picture, of course, but either or even both together do not necessarily constitute saving faith. A person can be convinced in his head of the existence of God. You can hem a man in until he has to admit there must be a God. But one thinks of the expression "A man convinced against his will is of the same opinion still."

What about the will? A man may desire to believe that Jesus has been raised from the dead. But his desire, his most fervent wish, will not save him. He may have a strong motivation. He may be utterly sincere. He may even be "willing to be willing." He might even take the existential view of faith—the "leap." He may say to himself, "I hope it's so." But all that may fall short of the *heart*.

That leads us to the object of faith. It is believing that Jesus was raised from the dead. Thus the supernatural element comes into focus. One either believes in Jesus' resurrection or one doesn't. It will not do for a person to play games with himself. He knows whether he actually believes that Jesus rose from the dead. One does not need to tell him whether he believes it. He does or he doesn't and he knows whether he *really* believes it or if he does not. If he does *not* believe in the resurrection of Jesus, there is nothing that will save him. He can resolve to be a better person, to live a moral life, respect God's Law, His people, His church and His ministers. He can even begin to feel sorry for bad things he has done and try to put them right. He can "quit his sinning." But if he does not believe in the resurrection of Jesus from the dead, he cannot be saved.

At this particular time in history Romans 10:9 is of special significance. For we are in an age of unbelief in a way that is different from previous ages. That is largely due to the emergence of modern scientific rationalism. Belief in the supernatural is not "in." The emergence of science, psychology, linguistic philosophy, sociology, and Marxism militate against belief in the supernatural in a way that previous generations have not had to combat. For example, two hundred years ago there was almost an uncritical acceptance of the resurrection of Jesus Christ. People often thought they just had to believe it—and did. Or did they? They thought they did. My point is this: believing in the resurrection of Jesus as we approach the end of the twentieth century shows an undoubted contrast with the spirit of our age. We have an opportunity to demonstrate, in a way previous generations were not as challenged to do, that we really believe in the living God.

The object of saving faith is the resurrection of Jesus. That is, that Jesus of Nazareth—the man who died a horrible death on the cross—was raised to life in the same body He had had since His birth. It was a spiritual body, yes. But it was also the same body. The tomb in which He was laid was empty save for His grave clothes (John 20:7). The resurrected Jesus said to Thomas (who seems to have sulked a bit for having missed seeing Jesus when the other disciples did), "Reach hither thy finger, and behold my hands; and reach hither thy hand, and thrust it into my side (John 20:27). What Thomas had demanded was the "print of the nails" (John 20:25). He got his evidence. My point again is this: we are talking about the raising of Jesus' very body. This

27

historical event—the resurrection of Jesus of Nazareth from the dead on the third day after His crucifixion—is the *object* of saving faith.

But someone will surely ask, "Why haven't you stressed trusting Jesus' death on the cross as the object of faith?" Or we might ask: "Why didn't Paul say, 'If thou shalt confess with thy mouth the Lord Jesus, and shalt believe in thine heart that he died on the cross for your sins, thou shalt be saved.'" There are good reasons for this.

First, Paul had reached the stage in the epistle to the Romans where his argument for justification by faith alone was beyond question. He in fact stated unequivocally that the death of Jesus is the object of saving faith. He said this at the beginning of his argument on the nature of justification. We are saved "through faith in his blood" (Romans 3:25). God set forth Jesus Christ as a *propitiation* through faith in His blood. Propitiation is a synonym for atonement. It simply means that God has been *appeased* by Christ's sacrifice. In other words, then, Paul had already stated in this same epistle that the object of faith is the death of Jesus (cf. Romans 5:9,10 11, 17, 18, 19; 6:3, 10; 7:4; 8:3, 34).

But in Romans 10, Paul anticipated the question whether one must ascend to heaven ("to bring Christ down from above") or descend into the deep ("to bring up Christ again from the dead") in order to know that one will be saved. The theme in these verses is "the righteousness which is of faith"" (Romans 10: 6-7). We would likely call it the *nature of faith*, that is, saving faith. Paul therefore reached this conclusion: you need not ascend to heaven or descend to the abyss. "But what saith it? The word is *nigh* thee, even in thy mouth, and in thy heart that is, the word of faith, which we preach" (Romans 10:8). You just believe in your *heart* Thomas had a firsthand experience of the resurrected Jesus. But Jesus said to Thomas, "Because thou hast seen me, thou hast believed: blessed are they that have not seen, and yet have believed" (John 20 29). That means us.

But there is another reason Paul said that the object of saving faith is Jesus' resurrection. It is because one need not have an articulate grasp of the doctrine of justification by faith in order to be saved. The Pauline doctrine of justification by faith is profound. It is so profound that one learns something new nearly every time one reads Romans or Galatians. Even Martin Luther did not perceive many of the implications of his own insight. John Calvin is much clearer on justification by faith than Luther. Luther nonetheless was able to see something in Paul's teaching that had escaped the notice of such great men as Athanasius, Augustine, Aquinas, and Anselm! Are we to say that these four great men will not be in heaven.? No! Of course not. Thus when Paul came to the *summary* of his teaching of justification and the nature of faith, he put his position in such a manner that anybody can be saved who believes in Jesus' resurrection and deity. The work of the Spirit takes care of this. All one needs to do, then, is truly to believe that Jesus was raised from the dead and confess that He is Lord.

It is an important reminder that we are not saved by how much we know. This is of immense importance. It does not take a lot of knowledge to be saved. What matters is whether a work of the Spirit has taken place that indicates a person has believed in his heart what the natural man could not possibly affirm.

On the day of Pentecost the great theme was the resurrection of Jesus, not the forgiveness of sins. Believing and confessing that Jesus was raised from the dead was what mattered. When the men cried out to Peter, "What shall we do?" Peter brought in the matter of repentance, baptism, forgiveness of sins, and the gift of the Holy Spirit - four important doctrines. But it was not required that the hearers fully understand these truths. They were baptised the very same day and it is not likely that there was time for much instruction. They had only accepted the fact that Jesus of Nazareth was raised from the dead! Peter told them to repent, that is, to agree with God. There is no indication here that these men were convicted of wickedness insofar as immorality and the works of the law were concerned. Their unbelief lay in their view about Jesus. They had to repent of that. They had been wrong. They had to turn about face and admit this.

Repentance is an essential ingredient in saving faith. The Greek word is *metanoia*, which means "change of mind." But we must be cautious here. I think it is possible to carry the idea of change of mind too far and expect sainthood before conversion! It is being sorry for one's past sins. It is an attitude of the heart. Repentance is therefore an assumption in Romans 10:9-10.

On the day of Pentecost repentance was therefore required. Not only that - they had to confess this repentance. Baptism was the way it was done on that occasion. But there was more - forgiveness of sins came into being. We cannot say that forgiveness of sins was even on their minds before that moment but forgiveness of sins is what they got. On top of all that came the promise of the Holy Spirit. All this is found in Acts 2:37-38. In a word: by believing and confessing the resurrection of Jesus three thousand men received forgiveness of sins and justification before God as an unexpected bonus! It follows for the apostle Paul that confessing Jesus as Lord and believing in the heart that He was raised from the dead constitutes an infallible guarantee of salvation.

The question may arise, then why not stress the resurrection of Jesus today rather than His death on the cross? The answer is, belief in either puts the other into effectual operation. It would not matter which is stressed. Paul spent most of his time on the nature of justification by faith in Jesus' blood but in the end he simply concluded that believing in the resurrection was sufficient. For if you believe in your heart that Jesus was raised from the dead and confess Jesus as Lord, you have *all* that Paul was arguing for - even if you don't understand Paul himself. As three thousand got more than they could have imagined at the time, so do we have in Christ infinitely more than we have ever dreamed of. Bible study can be defined as trying to catch up with our conversion. Bible study is finding out what really happened when we were saved.

As for the person who is converted by focusing his gaze upon the death of Christ, one may be absolutely certain he will also believe in Christ's resurrection . It would be just as impossible to believe that faith in Christ's blood saves and not also to believe in His resurrection as it would be to believe in His resurrection and not have the benefit of His blood. Anybody who believes that the death of God's son propitiated the Father will find it easier, as it were, to believe in our Lord's resurrection.

It is likely that the main reason today's Christianity (at least in the West) sometimes emphasises the death of Christ more than His resurrection is because we have a clearer knowledge of justification by faith as a legacy of the Reformation. Romans and Galatians (and, for that matter, the whole of the New Testament) is clearer to us than it was for many Christians before Luther's time. Moreover, as Paul spent so much time working out the details of the nature of justification through Jesus' death, surely we are "justified" in focusing upon this aspect of Bible doctrine. For the one who understands it, the reward is truly great. There is every reason we should *begin* with forgiveness of sins through the death of Christ in our evangelism and our understanding of the gospel. The epistle to the Romans most certainly encourages this approach.

But the danger of this approach is very real. To the man who has a keen grasp of doctrine like propitiation, atonement, justification, imputation, righteousness. forgiveness, and faith, there may be an impatience with the one who does not have such theological perception. This impatience can lead to intolerance and, in some cases, judgmentalism that questions whether a person can truly be a Christian if he does not understand such doctrines.

If the great apostle Paul could work so hard at defining his doctrine in several chapters in Romans and then say, at the end of it all, that heart belief in Christ's resurrection saves a man (if he confesses Christ as

Lord), surely we can afford to be as magnanimous ourselves?

2

What Do We Mean By Saved?

In the first chapter we examined the first part of our statement of the doctrine of once saved always saved. In this chapter we will take up the second part of that statement: [whoever] *confesses that Jesus is Lord will go to heaven when he dies*. We are resting our case almost entirely upon Romans 10:9-10, yet obviously our interpretation of those verses must absolutely co-here with every other Scripture or we would be violating a fundamental principle of Bible study. One must never build one's case on a single verse in the Bible outside its context. If our interpretation of a verse is right in line with its immediate context, you may be sure that it will fit perfectly with the rest of Scripture. The Bible does not contradict itself. If a verse in its context is set alongside other verses in their context, there is a magnificent coherence that further attests the infallibility of the Bible.

Paul's statement in Romans 10:9 demands two things in order that a person may be sure he has saving faith: first, that he believes in his heart that Jesus was raised from the dead; second, that he confesses that Jesus is

Lord. "That if thou shalt confess with thy mouth the Lord Jesus, and shalt believe in thine heart that God hath raised him from the dead, thou shalt be saved." One may enquire as to the order of the two. Romans 10:9 puts the confession first. Romans 10:10 puts heart belief first. "For with the heart man believeth unto righteousness; and with the mouth confession is made unto salvation." Which in fact comes first? Answer: the belief of the heart. For it will do no good to confess that Jesus is Lord if one does not *already* believe that Jesus has risen from the dead. Paul's own order of salvation is actually stated in Romans 10:10. It is faith that comes first. We believe before we do. This is not always true once a person is truly saved. For obedience can determine spiritual growth after we have been saved. But insofar as the way of salvation is concerned, believing comes before doing.

And yet there is a *doing* that is required before assurance of salvation emerges. This doing Paul calls "confession. "It is confessing "the Lord Jesus." ("Jesus is Lord," NIV). The question may be asked: Is it really possible to believe in one's heart that Jesus has been raised from the dead and then *refuse* to confess Him as Lord? I can give a biblical example that attests that this is truly possible. There were guards at the tomb when Jesus was raised from the dead. How much they truly witnessed (whether they saw Jesus actually rise) is not known. But what is undoubted is that they knew He had been raised. They knew that Jesus' disciples had nothing to do with the tomb being empty. They knew it in their hearts. They actually told this to the authorities—the chief priests. There is every reason to believe that the chief priests believed the soldiers' word. For when news

36

of the soldiers' report reached the Sanhedrin (the body of men that approved Jesus' execution), they called a meeting. Did they confess Jesus as Lord? No. Did the soldiers themselves confess Jesus as Lord? No. Instead the soldiers accepted a pay-off to keep quiet about what they knew to be a fact.

> And when they [the chief priests] were as-
> sembled with the elders, and had taken coun-
> sel, they gave large money unto the soldiers,
> saying, Say ye, His disciples came by night,
> and stole him away while we slept. And if
> this come to the governors ears, we will
> persuade him, and secure you. So they took
> the money, and did as they were taught: and
> this saying is commonly reported among the
> Jews until this day. (Matthew 28:12-15)

Thus, believing in the supernatural is not sufficient to constitute saving faith. One day Peter and John decided to go into the temple. As they were coming into the entrance known as the Beautiful Gate there was a lame man, over forty years old but an invalid from birth, who was miraculously healed. Peter said to this man (who had hoped to receive alms), "Silver and gold have I none; but such as I have give I thee: in the name of Jesus Christ of Nazareth rise up and walk" (Acts 3:6). The man stood up and began "walking, and leaping, and praising God" (Acts 3:8). This man was well known, being a regular "attraction" to all who went into the temple by that gate. The word spread. The religious authorities heard about it and witnessed this man walking around. They confessed to the miracle. "A notable miracle hath been done ... and we cannot deny it" (Acts

4:16). They confessed to the miracle but they did not confess that Jesus is Lord.

I am certain that much the same thing can be said of Jesus' death on the cross. One can carefully explain why Jesus died, that He took our punishment and that it was for our sins that He was crucified. I have done this hundreds of times and, in many cases, have known people to believe what I said. But they refused to *confess* Jesus as Lord. I have been in people's homes and shared the gospel with them, bringing them right up to the point of asking them to confess Jesus Christ as Lord, but they would not do it. They agreed with everything I said. But they would not confess Him.

This is why the apostle Paul said "if." He made salvation depend on two conditions: belief and confession must come together. There is no saving faith unless *both* are present. That is a part of the scandal of the Christian faith. Some think that just because Christ died for all, then all must be saved. But as Calvin put it, that is precisely why Paul said what he did in Romans 10:9-10. In rather strong language John Calvin said that this "clearly proves the stupidity of the argument of certain interpreters who maintain that all are elected without distinction, because the doctrine of salvation is universal, and because God invites all men to Himself without distinction. The general nature of the promises does not alone and of itself make salvation common to all." All are invited, but not all respond. Those who do respond will be saved; those who do not will be lost. Calvin's words are particularly relevant to those who would make Christianity into a sophisticated system of universal redemption that does not require individual faith.

There is an unavoidable scandal to this gospel. It is not fashionable. Jesus said, "He that believeth and is baptized shall be saved; but he that believeth not shall be damned" (Mark 16:16).

The question may be asked, Is it possible to confess Jesus as Lord but not believe that He was raised from the dead? Yes, that is to confess superficially. I fear this has happened thousands of times. A person may confess with his mouth "Jesus is Lord" but not bother with the matter of Jesus' resurrection. As a matter of fact it is quite fashionable in some circles to proclaim Jesus as Lord. I have known many who have done this but who did not actually care whether He was raised from the dead. I have known many who have proclaimed Jesus as Lord but who deny that His death on the cross was a propitiation for our sins. How can people do that? They do it because Jesus is very important to them—that is, the human Jesus; the "historical" Jesus. They admire Jesus. Some would say they love Him and that is why they follow Him. But in actual fact Jesus is little more than a hero to them. They admire His teachings (some of them) and claim to love His example. That is how they can proclaim Him as Lord.

It is because Paul anticipated a divorcing of the two elements in this dichotomy that he added, "*And* shalt believe in thine heart that God hath raised him from the dead, thou shalt be saved" (Romans 10:9). For it is not enough to say Jesus is Lord. It is not enough to make a profession of faith, even if it is in front of thousands. It is not enough to come forward or walk up an aisle, even if it is in front of thousands. It is not enough to be baptised, even if it is in front of thousands. There is nothing sacramental about a confession.

The reader should have seen by this time precisely why we must emphasise the whole of Romans 10:9-10. Confession and heart belief go together. One without the other renders faith invalid. At this stage our aforementioned definition will bear closer examination.

And *confesses*. In the two verses (Romans 10:9-10) Paul mentions the mouth twice. "If thou shalt confess with thy mouth . . . with the mouth confession is made." A person must *tell it* if he trusts the Lord Jesus Christ. "Let the redeemed of the Lord say so" (Psalm 107:2). Jesus Himself said, "Whosoever therefore shall confess me before men, him will I confess also before my Father which is in heaven. But whosoever shall deny me before men, him will I also deny before my Father which is in heaven" (Matthew 10:32-33). It is as though confessing ratifies our salvation. It validates it. It sets it into operation.

The ancient manner of confession was baptism. Baptism sent a signal to Caesar (or anyone else) that one was not ashamed of Jesus. There was a great stigma in being baptised.It was done in the presence of others and it served notice that the participant had come out of hiding! "Whosoever therefore shall be ashamed of me and of my words in this adulterous and sinful generation; of him also shall the Son of man be ashamed, when he cometh in the glory of his Father with the holy angels" (Mark 8:38). What takes place secretly in the heart must be made open before men.

The question probably follows, "What if a person is not actually baptised?" Will he be lost if he believes in his heart that God raised Jesus from the dead but is not

40

baptised? Answer: the thief on the cross was not baptized but he confessed Jesus as Lord. Moments before he died he said to Jesus, "Lord, remember me when thou comest into thy kingdom." And Jesus said unto him, "Verily I say unto thee, Today shalt thou be with me in paradise" (Luke 23:42-43). There was no opportunity for baptism. But this man was saved. His confession ratified it, as it were. He saw Jesus as sinless and himself as guilty. "We receive the due reward of our deeds: but this man hath done nothing amiss" (Luke 23:41). Not only that, but his saying that he wanted to be remembered when Jesus came into His kingdom was actually confessing Christ's resurrection. How else could the thief have known that Christ would come into His kingdom? A supernatural work of the Spirit brought about this insight. Moreover, he called Jesus "Lord." "No man can say that Jesus is the Lord, but by the Holy Ghost" (1 Corinthians 12:3).

The confession that is intended is with the mouth. Why the mouth? So that it can be heard. God already sees the heart, therefore it is not a confession to God here that is intended. It is a confession before men. Baptism is a visible matter. People can see it. But it does not follow that everyone must *see* one's confession. When Jesus said, "He that believeth and is baptised shall be saved," He was not saying that one must be baptised to be saved. Baptism in Mark 16:16 said the same things as confession. This is why Paul emphasized the mouth. Mark 16:16 cannot contradict Luke 23:43 (assurance to the thief on the cross) and this may be why the latter half of Mark 16:16 omits the reference to baptism: "But he that believeth not shall be damned." The main thing is to *tell it* once you have come to believe in Jesus. Tell it to at least one other person. Such a confession likewise says the same thing as baptism! And yet I would urge that one should be baptised at the earliest possible time for this dignifies the ordinance which Jesus gave to the Church. It is a beautiful demonstration that one truly is not ashamed to be utterly identified with Jesus' death and resurrection.

What if a person is alone, or speechless, on his death bed but finally believes the promise of the gospel? My answer: God sees the heart and knows that such a person most certainly would confess Christ openly if he had an opportunity. I would not be surprised to see thousands of people in heaven who called on the name of the Lord in their hearts just before they died. After all, Paul gave this simple promise as well in Romans 10:13: "For whosoever shall call upon the name of the Lord shall be saved." God is rich in mercy (Ephesians 2:4). It is God who gives faith in the first place, and if someone believes at the last minute, I do not believe that God would mock that person by granting faith at one moment then refusing entrance into heaven the next.

But, as Spurgeon put it, we have only *one* example of a deathbed conversion in the New Testament (the thief on the cross). We do have one "that none may despair, but only one that none dare presume". The thief on the cross is a basis of comfort for those of us who fervently hope for some of our loved ones whose final condition we are not sure about. But the thief on the cross is no example for those of us who are alive and well.

That Jesus is Lord. The nature of the confession is this: Jesus is Lord. What is at stake here is the vindication of God's name and honour. The confession that Jesus is Lord is our opportunity to beat the rest of the world to the draw. For the whole world will one day openly confess that Jesus is Lord. The Christian does it now. In a word, we clear God's honour and name by faith—now. In the Final Day everybody will do it. "As I live, saith the Lord, every knee shall bow to me, and every tongue shall confess to God" (Romans 14:11). "Wherefore God also hath highly exalted him, and given him a name which is above every name: that at the name of Jesus every knee should bow, of things in heaven, and things in earth, and things under the earth; and that every tongue should confess that Jesus Christ is Lord, to the glory of God the Father" (Philippians 2:9-11).

It is not a question of *whether* men will confess that Jesus is Lord—it is only a question of *when*. They will do it now voluntarily or someday involuntarily. They will do it now willingly or they will do it then unwillingly. They will do it now by faith or they will do it on the Last Day by sight. Today God uses persuasion. One day He will use force. Men may win the battle, but God will win the war. "Every knee shall bow and every tongue shall confess that Jesus Christ is Lord."

The confession that all men will utter at God's final judgment is precisely the confession they are called to make in the here and now. It has to do with one's view of Jesus. Who is He? "What think ye of Christ? whose Son is he?" (Matthew 22:42). When Jesus asked the Pharisees the question, "If David then call him Lord, how is he his son?" (Matthew 22:45), it was Jesus' own affirmation that He was the Son of God and God the Son.

"And no man was able to answer him a word, neither durst any man from that day forth ask him any more questions" (Matthew 22:46). The Pharisees got the message. The message is the same: Jesus is God. "In the beginning was the Word, and the Word was with God, and the Word was God . . . and the Word was made flesh, and dwelt among us (and we beheld his glory, the glory as of the only begotten of the Father) full of grace and truth" John 1:1, 14). Jesus was man as though He were not God, yet God as though He were not man. He was fully God, fully man. God called Jesus "God": "But unto the Son he saith, Thy throne, O God, is for ever and ever: a sceptre of righteousness is the sceptre of thy kingdom" (Hebrews 1:8). John called Jesus Christ "the true God" (1 John 5:20) for He is God. "And he is before all things, and by him all things consist . . . For it pleased the Father that in him should all fulness dwell" (Colossians 1:17, 19). "For in him dwelleth all the fulness of the Godhead bodily" (Colossians 2:9).

There are some who will not confess that Jesus is Lord, but Paul gives the reason for this. "No man can say that Jesus is the Lord, but by the Holy Ghost" (1 Corinthians 12:3). This further demonstrates that the confession "Jesus is Lord" is an affirmation of Christ's deity and honour, not esteeming Him as a kind of hero or great leader. I repeat there are those who will proclaim Jesus as Lord who do not even believe in His bodily resurrection or deity. It does not require the work of the Holy Spirit to call Jesus "Lord" if by that a kind of heroic admiration is meant. What requires the Spirit in such a confession is the affirmation that Jesus is *God*. This is what Paul meant. To Paul there was no difference. The

Lord is God. God is the Lord. Therefore one must not only believe in Jesus' resurrection but His deity. Saving faith, then, consists of an affirmation both of Christ's person and His work. The affirmation begins in the heart but it must come out through the mouth. What comes out of the mouth is an unashamed affirmation of *who Jesus is*. He is Lord. He is God. Sovereign Ruler. King. Almighty God. Creator. Such is Jesus.

The question may be asked whether everyone who confesses "Jesus is Lord" understands all he is saying. The question might be put better were we to ask, "Does *anyone* understand all he is saying when he confesses "Jesus is Lord?" Hardly. Who among us fully understands this now? What seasoned saint would dare step forward to claim he understands everything that phrase means? Yet Paul puts the confession in the simplest of terms that we might be assured by just a glimpse into the glory of the Son of God. It was enough that the eunuch of Ethiopia confessed, "I believe that Jesus Christ is the Son of God" (Acts 8:37). That was saying the same thing as "Jesus is Lord." Peter ended his sermon on the day of Pentecost with these words: "Therefore let all the house of Israel know assuredly, that God hath made that same Jesus, whom ye have crucified, both Lord and Christ" (Acts 2:36). Thus when his hearers cried out, "What shall we do?" it was obvious that these people were ready to do *anything*. They were baptised the same day. It was a way of confessing that Peter had gotten it right. Most certainly they knew a lot more ten days later, and ten months later, and ten years later, than they grasped on the day they were baptised. But they were saved on that very day. Why? They were faithful in that which is "least" (Luke 16:10). God doesn't lead us directly from A to Z - He leads us rather from A to B, and from B to C. The confession that is required is to *agree with God.* That is the essence of repentance - agreeing with what God says. On the day of Pentecost three thousand agreed with Peter and they were baptised immediately.

Will go to heaven when he dies. Whoever once truly believes that Jesus was raised from the dead, and confesses that Jesus is Lord, will go to heaven when he dies. "Once saved, always saved" means that such a person cannot lose his salvation. It follows, then, that he will go to heaven when he dies. It is an absolute enforceable promise. We are not saying once saved, always obedient. We are not saying once saved, always perfect. We are not saying once saved, always godly. It is once saved, always *saved.*

We now come to the heart of the matter of being saved. What do we mean by *saved?* There has been a trend away from the term *saved.* Some are embarrassed by it. I'm not sure when the trend began, but there seems to have been an effort made by some to destigmatise the heart of the Christian faith by using terms that are slightly more sophisticated. Thus being *saved* seems to have been changed to being *converted.* But eventually that term seemed a bit too old-fashioned so people began to talk about being *committed.*

But the biblical term is *saved.* It is found no fewer than forty seven times in the New Testament alone. The verb *save is* found no fewer than twenty-five times in the New Testament. Admittedly not every single usage fits the doctrine on which this book is centered. But most of them do. That is precisely why Jesus is called Saviour.

"Thou shalt call his name JESUS: for he shall *save* his people from their sins" (Matthew 1:21). "For unto you is born this day in the city of David a Saviour, which is Christ the Lord" (Luke 2:11). "He *saved* others; himself he cannot save," shouted the chief priests at the scene of Jesus' cross (Mark 15:31). "Wherefore he is able also to *save* them to the uttermost that come unto God by him, seeing he ever liveth to make intercession for them" (Hebrews 7:25). "Sirs, what must I do to be saved?" cried the Philippian jailer. Paul and Silas answered, "Believe on the Lord Jesus Christ, and thou shalt be *saved,* and thy house" (Acts 16:30-31). Peter proclaimed, "Neither is there *salvation* in any other: for there is none other name under heaven given among men, whereby we must be *saved*" (Acts 4:12).

Our basic term, then, is biblical. The verses in the preceding paragraph indicate more than one usage of our term *saved.* A subsequent section will attempt to deal with the ways the term *saved is* used. But as we are only stating our doctrine at this stage, not necessarily trying to defend it, we will put the bottom line of the teaching right here: Saved means that one is preserved from hell. To be saved is to go to heaven when you die.

"Once saved, always saved" means that being saved is an unchangeable position. It cannot be changed in this life, not to mention the age to come. It is an irrevocable gift from God. My wife recently revealed to me how she first heard the phrase "once saved, always saved." It was a number of years ago when we were in college, at an institution of our former denomination. The young lady who was to be my wife but who at the time had not met me was going through a spiritual crisis. She found

47

herself questioning some of the theological views that she was told that she had to accept. But when her friends saw they were not able to help her, one of them said to her, "You should talk to R. T. Kendall. He believes in once saved, always saved." My wife said to herself, "That couldn't be right, but isn't that a lovely expression and a wonderful thought?" Her problem, as with so many, was that the idea seemed too good to be true.

But it is true. Once we truly grasp the gospel and the nature of God's promise, we see that it is the only way it could be. We blush that we could have ever doubted it.

It is a thing most wonderful
Almost too wonderful to be,
That God's own Son should come from heaven
And die to save a child like me.

W. W. How

3

A Sweet Clarification

There are many interpreters of Scripture who may agree essentially with what I have stated up to now. Indeed, it is likely that a majority of evangelical Christians would be happy to subscribe to the statement of doctrine I outlined near the beginning of our first chapter. But it will be recalled that I added a P. S., as it were, to that statement: *Such a person will go to heaven when he dies no matter what work (or lack of work) may accompany such faith.*

Many proponents of the doctrine of the eternal security of the believer often look the other way when certain questions arise - some water down the doctrine. But let us be fair with them. They are aware of the preponderance of biblical injunctions to holy living. They want to dignify such scriptural commands. They therefore are hesitant to draw certain conclusions that may be derived from the doctrine we have sought to define. Indeed such questions and conclusions are fairly obvious. All of us have thought of them. But we sometimes get uneasy in discussing them.

Either the doctrine is true or it is not. If it is true, it is only because it is totally and consistently biblical. If it is biblical, then there is nothing whatsoever to worry about. The conclusions that we may draw from the doctrine would also have been drawn by the biblical writers. Those writers were compassionate men. We may safely affirm that they were not only men with theological sense but men with common sense. They thought of *all* of the objections we could think of. But did they water down their teaching?

It is one thing to write a theological treatise while sitting in an ivory tower, but quite another to live with real people and listen to their questions. None of the biblical writers lived in an ivory tower. They were not only theologians, they were pastors. Peter said, "The elders which are among you I exhort, who are also an elder" (1 Peter 5:1, "I appeal as a fellow elder," NIV). It is not unusual to see the apostle Paul as a theologian, but the genius that lay behind the great apostle Paul was that he was essentially an evangelist and pastor. "I write not these things to shame you," he once said to the Christians at Corinth, "but as my beloved sons I warn you. For though ye have ten thousand instructors in Christ, yet have ye not many fathers for in Christ Jesus I have begotten you through the gospel" (1 Corinthians 4:1415). We may be sure that any question that emerged in our minds as to the doctrine of the eternal security of the believer was asked *of* the New Testament writers and *by* them. We need have no fear in putting to the biblical writers questions that enter into our minds.

"What if we sin?" That is the most obvious question. This question is then often reshaped and put like this: "What if a person who is saved falls into sin, stays in sin, and is found in that very condition when he dies? Will he still go to heaven?" The answer is yes. If he was truly saved in the first place, yes. If the answer to the question is no, then this book is utterly unnecessary. For if the matter of sin did not enter the picture, there would be no problem at all. There would never be a need for the doctrine of eternal security and there would never be an objection to it. We therefore will not proceed further in this book until we have made this clarification—a most delightful clarification.

A common way of dealing with this matter is to say, "If they fall into sin, it shows they were never saved." There are however a number of interpreters who would be willing to go further and say, "They may have been saved, but if they are truly saved, they will repent." The common way out of this dilemma, then, is to say, "If they do not eventually repent, it shows that they were never saved in the first place." This kind of thinking reflects a lack of belief in the very gospel on which our doctrine rests. The premise for people like this is: if John Smith is saved, he will show it; if he doesn't show it, he wasn't saved. To show it usually means living a life of consistent godliness.

As we shall clearly see later in this book, the present writer has no intention of painting a doctrinal picture that encourages sin. I only hope the reader will examine the *entire* book most carefully. But at this stage I simply want to face the matter which all of us think about (but are so often afraid to talk about). For if there is the *slightest possibility* that a saved person can ever be lost, the doctrine affords no comfort to me whatever. For I would constantly be worried about that slightest possibility being relevant to me. To put it another way, if it were stated that 99 percent of saved people cannot be lost but one percent could lose their salvation, I would be in perpetual and total fear that I would be among the one percent. For I would need to know what kind of sin or disobedience it is that catches the one percent. Whatever such a sin or disobedience may be, I would live in constant horror that I just might—someday—commit such a sin.

For I am no different from anybody else. All temptation is "common to man" (1 Corinthians 10:13). Whatever sin has been committed at any time in human history could be committed by me, given certain circumstances. I am no different. I am by nature a child of wrath, "even as others" (Ephesians 2:3). That means that in me lies the potential for the greatest or most extreme sin that has ever been conceived by a wicked heart.

Therefore the security of 99 percent of all saved people being assured of never going to hell would give me no more comfort than the possibility that 50 percent are so assured—or one percent. I need to know whether Jesus meant it for every believer when he said, "And I give them eternal life; and they shall never perish, neither shall any man pluck them out of my hand" John 10:28). Indeed, "no man is able to pluck them out of my Father's hand" John 10:29). I need equally to know that Paul meant it for every believer when he said, "For I am persuaded, that neither death, nor life, nor angels, nor principalities, nor powers, nor things present, nor things to come, nor height, nor depth, nor any other creature, shall be able to separate us from the love of God, which is in Christ Jesus our Lord" (Romans 8:38-39).

I therefore state categorically that the person who is saved—who confesses that Jesus is Lord and believes in his heart that God raised Him from the dead will *go to heaven when he dies no matter what work (or lack of work) may accompany such faith*. In other words, no matter what sin (or absence of Christian obedience) may accompany such faith.

Some may feel that to be so candid is unbecoming to the gospel. It is not. It is precisely what honours it. For that is what makes the gospel an offense-a scandal (Gr. *skandalon*—1 Corinthians 1:23, a "stumbling block"). Some may feel that this is dragging a skeleton out of the cupboard that is better left inside. But wait a minute. All of us are by nature full of dead men's bones, being no different from the Pharisees (Matthew 23:27). There is not a single one of us who does not at times have secret thoughts that are heinous and horrifying. *All* of us need to know that there is *nothing* we can ever do that could separate us from the love of God. What the gospel does is to assure us that we are saved, eternally saved, by sheer grace, through faith alone.

It is because we believe in salvation by grace through faith without works that we can rest our case so confidently. The gospel on which "once saved, always saved" rests is by grace, through faith alone. It is not quite correct to say by grace alone— full stop. The reason is this: Paul said we are saved "by grace through faith" (Ephesians 2:8). It is by grace, yes, but also through faith. Were we to leave out faith and call it grace only then there would be no need for evangelism. Whereas Paul did say that God was in Christ, reconciling the world unto himself (2 Corinthians 5:19), he immediately added that we are ambassadors for Christ, as though God did beseech you by us: we pray you in Christ's stead, be ye reconciled to God" (2 Corinthians 5:20). In other words, the gospel demands faith. The gospel is not merely "Christ died for you" but "*believe* that He died for you." It is therefore grace offered upon the *condition* of faith. Hence Paul's little word *if* in Romans 10:9. If a person does not *believe* that Christ died for him, it becomes grace that was rejected, not received. The gospel must be received. It is a gift (Romans 6:23) but a gift must be accepted. "But as many as received him, to them gave he power to become the sons of God, even to them that believe on his name" John 1:12).

"Once saved, always saved" rests on the gospel of grace through faith—but faith *alone!* It is by grace through faith, but faith only. "Not of works, lest any man should boast" (Ephesians 2:9). We have been saved and given a calling "not according to our works, but according to his own purpose and grace, which was given us in Christ Jesus before the world began" (2 Timothy 1:9). "Not by works of righteousness which we have done, but according to his mercy he saved us, by the washing of regeneration, and renewing of the Holy Ghost" (Titus 3:5). "Being justified freely by his grace through the redemption that is in Christ Jesus: whom God hath set forth to be a propitiation *through faith in his blood*, to declare his righteousness for the remission of sins that are past, through the forbearance of God" (Romans 3:24-25).

In a word: grace is offered to all on the condition of

faith confessed but no condition *follows* such faith. John 3:16, which Martin Luther is said to have called "the gospel in a nutshell," shows the condition: "whosoever believeth." Thus to the person who believes there is given without any conditions whatever the assurance of everlasting life. Faith is "ratified" by our confession alone. There is nothing more required, insofar as assurance of heaven is concerned. If more were required, then we would have to say it is by grace through faith plus works - or by grace through faith on the condition of faithfulness. The stigma, or scandal, of the gospel of Jesus Christ is that heaven is offered to everyone who believes. Once a person has confessed his faith he is absolutely, unchangeably and irrevocably *saved*. Even if he doesn't believe in "once saved, always saved," he is still eternally secure nonetheless. Believing in the doctrine of eternal security is not what makes you eternally secure - it is the gospel that promises it.

To put it another way, it would be quite right to say that we are saved by grace alone, through faith alone, in Christ alone. For faith must have the correct object - Jesus Christ. Why is Christ the object of faith? It is because it is He who has done everything for us. We are putting our trust in Him - who He is and what He did. It is putting all our eggs in one basket, resting our faith, our lives, and our final destiny in *one man* - Jesus of Nazareth. Either His life and death atoned for our sins - or it did not. If it did, then we can rejoice with joy unspeakable and full of glory (1 Peter 1:8). If His sinless life and death on the cross in and by itself did not secure our eternal salvation, then, presumably, we must fill in the gap with good works. This book rests on the premise that the gospel means "good news." The news is that Christ alone, in and by Himself, satisfied God's eternal justice. All that is required of us is faith. Nothing more. That is the only reason we can affirm "once saved, always saved." If there were the slightest addition necessary to the death of Jesus on the cross, then we would have to reassess this entire teaching. We are resting our whole case on the finished work of Jesus Christ. All that is required of us in terms of works was provided by Him. "But of him are ye in Christ Jesus, who of God is made unto us wisdom, and righteousness, and sanctification, and redemption: that, according as it is written, He that glorieth, let him glory in the Lord" (1 Corinthians 1:3-31).

Let us look again at our P. S.: *Such a person will go to heaven when he dies no matter what work (or lack of work) may accompany such faith. It* may be justifiably argued that there is no such thing as a "lack of work" accompanying faith. For whatever behaviour or conduct may characterise the believer it can be called a work, whether good or bad. If I sin, it may be called a bad work, if I obey Christ's commands, it may be called a good work. For this reason "lack of work" is redundant. But I put it that way in order to make it absolutely clear that salvation is by grace through faith alone - faith plus nothing.

Good works do not help the slightest bit with reference to our eternal salvation. Once a person has rested his case in the finished work of Jesus Christ, there is nothing further he can do to help neither is there anything further he can do that can hurt. For living the most exemplary Christian life after one's conversion does not make a person "more certain" of going to heaven. If a person thinks that living the most consistent godly life will help him along a bit with respect to his salvation he betrays his lack of belief in Christ's atonement. Worst of all, such good works do not even avail in terms of the life of the Spirit, unless they are done in love. The reason is this: it is "faith which worketh by love" (Galatians 5:6) that truly edifies the soul and honours Christ, but the faith that works by fear is of no value. For this reason the person who thinks he could forfeit his own salvation by lack of obedience cannot obey the Lord apart from a motive of fear. He may *say* that he loves the Lord. But when he knows in his heart of hearts that there is the remotest possibility he could somehow be eternally lost, such good works at bottom are done in fear, not love. It is only when a person is absolutely convinced that he is going to heaven when he dies that a good work is of value. For it is then that he shows how much he loves the Lord. For the Lord knows whether we think such good works are done out of gratitude or done out of fear. It is works done in gratitude that please the Lord and that demonstrate our true love for Him. But if I know that I could lose my salvation in the absence of good works, I am going to make certain that those good works are there. Let me turn the previous sentence around: if I know I could lose my salvation owing to the presence of bad works (sin), I am going to make certain that such bad works do not emerge. Why? I don't want to be lost. I can tell myself that I expect to get to heaven by Jesus' blood, but if I entertain the remotest possibility that there is something I can do (or not do) that can nullify Jesus' blood, I will focus my attention on my obedience, not

Christ's blood. That is the way human nature works.

Thus the great pity for those who do not believe in "once saved, always saved" is that the very works they are trying so earnestly to produce do not help at all. They do not help with respect to their own salvation; they do not even help with respect to their inheritance in the life of the Spirit. Those who doubt lose all around. For it is faith that works by love that leads us deeper into the life of the Spirit. Faith that works by love is not possible to the one who has not put all his eggs into one basket—the finished work of Jesus on the cross.

And yet one can see why some call "once saved, always saved" a dangerous teaching. It is dynamite. It puts us on our honour. It sets us free. It is vulnerable to abuse. There is no doubt that it is a teaching that has been abused. It is perhaps the most abused teaching of the New Testament. The incestuous believer of Corinth abused it (1 Corinthians 5:1-5). But Paul stuck to his guns, not modifying his position the slightest bit. God knew that men would be tempted to abuse it when "in the wisdom of God the world by wisdom knew not God, it pleased God by the foolishness of preaching to save them that believe" (1 Corinthians 1:21). The gospel has always been vulnerable to the charge of antinomianism (literally: "against law"; the idea being it does not matter how you live). Martin Luther was accused of this, but so was Paul a long time before (Romans 3:8). And yet none of the New Testament writers watered the teaching down in order to protect the gospel from abuse.

The motive to live holy and godly lives must spring from love if such godliness is to be rewarded. By the way, *rewarded* is the right word. God rewards godliness, there is no doubt about that. But the reward is not salvation. It is knowing that you *have* salvation and that you cannot lose it which is the first qualification for the reward God delights to give. It is only when the matter of assurance of eternal salvation is, as it were, completely behind you that you are truly ready to move on in the Christian life. This is why this chapter has dealt with the question all of us think about, "What if we sin?" For we need to know that our salvation is free. Absolutely free.

> *Guilty, vile and helpless, we:*
> *Spotless Lamb of God was He:*
> *"Full atonement!" can it be?*
> *Hallelujah! what a Saviour!*

P. P. Bliss

4

Why Believe This Doctrine?

A jumbo jet with four hundred people was preparing to take off from London's Heathrow Airport. It taxied down the runway, eventually moving into position to assume full speed.

The engines roared, we were thrust back into our seats. The plane, though going faster and faster seemed never to get off the ground. One wondered if it would actually make it for it seemed an eternity before the plane's nose tilted heavenward. But just before the plane left the ground I noticed some passengers next to me who began lifting their feet off the floor. They were sure the plane needed all the help it could get!

That is the way many people live the Christian life. They do not rest in God. They take their feet off the floor, as it were, as if that will help God to take them to heaven. Their view is that, even if the doctrine of once saved, always saved is true, they still prefer to play it safe and live the Christian life as though this doctrine might not be true. After all, if it is true, they will be saved anyway - if it is not true, they hope to be sure they have enough good works to cushion their security.

In a slightly different vein I heard of a man in America who had been baptised thirteen times, including every conceivable mode of baptism: by immersion, by sprinkling, by pouring, by immersion three times forwards, by immersion three times backwards, etc. His rationale was this: One of them has got to be right. He didn't know which, but he was taking no chances.

Some people seek religion like those who play the stock market. For example, a man who has money to invest would not be likely to put all his money in one company. He would want the security of a broad range of investments, lest one stock go down. He plays it safe.

These illustrations point to the way many feel about the doctrine of once saved, always saved. Many love the idea (let no one doubt that) but they are simply afraid that it's not so. So, they play it safe. Indeed, I recently read an article on the subject, "Are Christians eternally secure? The writer's point was that the New Testament teaches an eternal security, but one which is conditional on continual faith and obedience. His reasoning was this: As our salvation is a conditional security (based upon continual faith and obedience), then all those who live according to its doctrine will be saved. But even if unconditional security is true, such faithful adherents will still be saved. Thus belief in and obedience to the teaching of *conditional* eternal security is the only spiritually *safe* way to live. In other words, this man was playing it safe.

The purpose of this chapter is to urge the reader to go for broke - to believe with all your heart that *Jesus paid it all*. Either He did, or He did not. If He did not, how could we ever be sure that we have sufficiently measured up to His standard of righteousness so that we may safely feel guarantied a home in heaven. ? Whether we are talking about *salvation* by works or *assurance* of salvation by works, the only standard is the law. Therefore, to feel the guarantee that we have a home in heaven by our obedience means that we have our work cut out for us! But, on the other hand, if Jesus fully paid the debt, we have nothing whatever to fear. If Jesus paid it all, I am saved. If He did not, I am in trouble.

By the way, are you afraid to do this? Are you truly afraid to put your total trust in the death of Jesus? Are you afraid that somehow God will still look to you for more payment after you have trusted His Son? Or are you afraid that the debt He paid in full can be recharged to you if you do not produce the works of the law? No man ever went to hell who trusted in the blood of God's beloved Son. But hell is full of people who trusted in their own self-righteousness.

I am aware of the responsibility I am undertaking in writing like this. I am not only putting my own soul on the line, but yours as well! I am literally asking you to rest your case where I have rested mine—in the death of Jesus. Believe me, His death *is all* I have going for me. I have no other hope.

> *My hope is built on nothing less*
> *Than Jesus' blood and righteousness;*
> *I dare not trust the sweetest frame,*
> *But wholly lean on Jesus' name.*

E. Mote

In other words, I am risking the possibility that some reader will take me absolutely seriously and trust in Jesus and no other. I entertain the possibility that someone will charge me with sending a person to hell. I certainly do not want to do that. But that is precisely how much I believe what this book is about. I have no fear of sending anybody to hell who will rest his eternal soul on the blood of Jesus.

I would now like to put this question to the reader: If Jesus in fact paid our debt in full, do you think that is something God *Himself* would want you to believe? Or would such knowledge be too dangerous? To put it another way, even if once saved, always saved is absolutely true, would God still want to hide that information from us? Would He keep that knowledge concealed from us in order to motivate us to a more careful walk with Him? Would God fear that if we really knew how much He loved us in Christ, it would be bad for us?

Let me ask you a question (if you are a parent): Do you want your own child to question your love for him (or her)? Are you afraid for your own child to know how much you really love him (or her)? Do you think it is more healthy for your child to feel there is some doubt about your love? Would you want your own child to feel the insecurity of being dislodged from your fatherly (or motherly) love?

Let me ask yet another question: How much would you *like* God to love you? How much could you wish that He loved you? If you could tell God how much you want Him to love you, how much would that be?

The same God who promises to answer our very prayers "above all that we ask or think" (Ephesians 3:20) and who puts before us possibilities that "eye hath not seen, nor ear heard" (1 Corinthians 2:9) loves us with a greater love than we can even conceive. How much would you *like* God to love you? That *is* how much He loves you - only more. How much could you *wish* that He loves you? That *is* how much He already loves you - only more. How much do you *want* Him to love you? That *is* how much He already loves you - only more.

He wants you to believe it. He wants you to believe Him, His own word! He does not play games with us. He does not conceal His love for us, as if He were courting us and playing it cool. We may try this act when courting a girlfriend or a boyfriend. But not God. The very thing He wants us to know is why He sent His Son and what it was His Son did. He does not want to conceal the minutest part of it lest we feel too secure. Absolute, eternal security is what He wants for us. That is why He has openly demonstrated His love by sending His Son. For us to turn around and question what this means comes perilously close to insulting Him. Not that we mean to insult Him. It is our unbelief that does it.

The devil knows what Jesus did on the cross. Jesus by His own blood "spoiled principalities and powers." He made "a shew of them openly, triumphing over them" by His cross (Colossians 2:15). God honours the blood of His Son; the devil hates it. The devil will do all he can do to divert people's attention from the blood of Jesus. It is not once saved, always saved of which the devil is the architect, it is any teaching that will lead to the slightest mistrust in the blood of Jesus shed on the cross. If you want to please God, honour the blood of His Son's cross. Plead it. Praise it. Trust it. It saves - utterly and completely.

What a pity that some Christians will find out when they get to heaven that they were eternally and irrevocably saved from the moment of their conversion, but spent their lives dialoguing with the devil over whether or not they were really saved. What a pity that many will find out in heaven there was no need for such insecurity and anxiety. What a pity that some will discover a truth they were afraid to believe on earth, but that would have given them peace, victory and a basis for solid growth in grace.

If we are going to find out that it is true in heaven, how much better that we discover it now. If it will be true then, it is true now. As a matter of fact we read in the book of Revelation that the praise of the Lamb is centered on this: "for thou wast slain, and hast redeemed us to God by thy blood" (Revelation 5:9). That is the message of heaven. Why should we wait until we are in heaven to believe it? God wants us to believe it now. It is His word. It is no secret. It is not hidden. It is not concealed. It is as dear as it can be.

Yes, this teaching has been abused. Yes, some may read this very book and abuse this teaching. But it is not my teaching. I am not the one who thought of it. I therefore do not apologise for it. I am sorry that it has been abused. I hope to make a small contribution on that very matter before this book is finished. But as for the doctrine itself, it is true - Jesus paid our debt in full.

> *Jesus paid it all,*
> *All to Him I owe;*
> *Sin had left a crimson stain,*
> *He washed it white as snow.*

Mrs. H. M. Hall

I now turn to substantial reasons for the reader to believe this teaching. I do not refer to the biblical defense at this stage as much as to the reasons you ought to believe it for your own sake. There is a sense in which I could call it *pragmatic* reasons for believing this teaching. In other words, you should believe it because it *works*. It is to your own advantage to believe it, and to your disadvantage not to believe it. I for the moment pass by the argument that you should believe it just because the Bible teaches it (you would expect me to say that). I put to the reader why this doctrine should and must be believed for your own sake.

IT IS THE ULTIMATE BASIS FOR PEACE

As long as there is the remotest possibility that the saved person could ever be lost, to that extent the door is opened for anxiety. As long as you entertain the possibility that, somehow or somewhere, you could sin so that you sever your relationship with God and risk being sent to hell, you cannot be at perfect peace. The whole time you are talking to God you are aware that the same God you are talking to will not be on speaking terms with you should you displease Him. Therefore *at bottom* when you are talking to Him you are aware that you hold the cards, as it were. It is ultimately up to you.

A subsidiary result of this is that you do not really respect God very much. You may not tell Him that. But you feel it, at least by repression (a defense mechanism whereby you deny what you feel). At bottom you are talking to a God whose power is limited by your faithfulness. Thus when you talk to God, you pray with tongue in cheek if you say anything about His faithfulness to you. What you really feel is your faithfulness to

Him. "Great is thy faithfulness" may come from your lips, but "Great is my faithfulness," comes from your heart. You therefore feel that you have earned the right to His goodness because you have been doing really well lately. In a word, it is not God you are really praising, it is yourself. (If you will be blushingly honest you will admit you have had these very thoughts before this moment.)

God does not want you to feel like that. But you cannot help it if you feel that you ultimately hold your own destiny in your hands. But if you knew - absolutely *knew* - that, whatever else may be true between now and the moment of your death, you would at least go to heaven when you die, your entire relationship with God would be radically affected. Nothing would ever be the same again. You would begin to praise Him, to adore Him, to stand in awe and wonder that God could be so merciful, and, dare I say it, you would be worshipping God indeed for the first time in your life. For a God who is any less than the one I have just described has difficulty in commanding the reverence and worship you would feel once you truly believed that your destiny is sealed by sheer grace and not works.

Once you know you are eternally saved, there is peace. I mean *peace*. That is why Paul could say, "Therefore being justified by faith, we have peace with God through our Lord Jesus Christ" (Romans 5:1). "For he is our peace" (Ephesians 2:14). "Having made peace through the blood of his cross" (Colossians 1:20). Such peace, as a matter of fact, is in operation anyway. For the blood of Jesus has effected it. But *enjoying* it for some Christians is quite another matter. There is a famous story that emerged shortly after the second world war. One remote island in the Pacific had not received word that the leaders of Japan had signed an unconditional surrender to General Douglas MacArthur on the Battleship Missouri in 1945. The result was that the fighting continued. There was a peace in operation but you couldn't have convinced anybody of that on this little island. So it is with those who do not enjoy what is actually true. If we have invited Jesus into our hearts, trusted His death on the cross, and confessed that He is Lord, God has declared the war over. How much better to learn that before we get to heaven. What a pity that the fighting still goes on.

Things are never the same again once you believe in your heart that nothing, absolutely nothing, can sever you from God once you are saved. There is that peace, the knowledge that you will some day go to heaven. Heaven is certain! You may backslide, you may sin, you may fall a thousand times and grieve the very Spirit of God whereby you are sealed unto the day of redemption (Ephesians 4:30), but you know nonetheless that you will go to heaven when you die. That brings peace. Peace.

Several years ago, driving in Fort Lauderdale, Florida, I put a proposition to my father. "Dad," I said, "Suppose Michael the archangel came down from heaven and told you that he happens to know you are eternally saved and that *you will be in heaven* when you die." "Oh, that would be wonderful," my father interrupted. Tears filled his eyes. "I'd rather know that than anything in the world." I then said, "Dad, I know that now." He replied, "I wish 1 did, son, but the Bible says in 1 Corinthians

10:12, 'Wherefore let him that thinketh he standeth take heed lest he fall.'" Then I said to my father, "But suppose Michael the archangel actually did tell you you are unconditionally, absolutely, and irrevocably saved. What effect do you suppose it would have on you? Would you want to go out and see how many sins you could commit?" "No," he immediately replied, "I must admit that I think the effect would be the opposite. I would be so thankful that I would want to live closer to the Lord than ever." That leads me to my next point.

IT IS THE ONLY FOUNDATION FOR TRUE GODLINESS

That may come as a surprise to some. But if it does sound surprising, it only betrays a faulty view of holiness. Many think that holiness is nothing more than keeping the works of the law. Many feel they ought to be congratulated if they abstain from adultery or lying or stealing. The truth is that it is possible to keep the works of the law externally and be not one inch closer to godliness. There are millions of people in the world today who are outwardly very moral. Some Hindus and Moslems are outwardly quite spotless. Even Paul claimed to be "blameless" before his conversion (Philippians 3:6). In Saudi Arabia, the drinking of an alcoholic beverage is forbidden and adultery is punishable by stoning. But would we be prepared to call this godliness?

Godliness is not possible until there is adequate conviction of sin. Such a conviction of sin is not possible until we have seen the glory of the Lord. The illustration of Isaiah should be sufficient to prove that. Here was a man who most likely was a very moral man. But one day he saw the glory of the Lord. The consequence of that sight was an overwhelming conviction of his own sin. "Woe is me!" he cried, "for I am undone; because . . . I dwell in the midst of a people of unclean lips: for mine eyes have seen the King, the Lord of hosts" (Isaiah 6:5). It was then that he was truly ready to be used of the Lord and be all that God wanted and needed. "I heard the voice of the Lord, saying, Whom shall I send, and who will go for us? Then said I, Here am I; send me" (Isaiah 6:8). It began with a sight of the glory of Christ.

Those who are afraid to rest their souls in the Lord Jesus alone have not seen His glory. And yet it does not mean they are not saved. As many imperfections surround our initial conversion and confession so do many people retain an abiding theological error that may persist all their lives. But were they truly to see the glory of the Lord, they would know how sinful they really are. Once we see how sinful we really are, we know that the only way we could possibly get to heaven would be by the sheer grace of God. Those who somehow think there is something they might yet do (or not do) that could change their standing in the grace of God betray a superficial view of sin. How could they imagine something as unreliable as our works could shape our eternal destiny? The amazing thing is that the blood cleanses us from *all* sin as we walk in the light (1 John 1:7), yet the light that we get is usually just enough for the next step towards true godliness. But the blood cleanses *all* sin, not merely the sin that is exposed by the next ray of God's light.

In a word, there can be no obedience that is God-owned until there is an unfeigned conviction of sin, and there can be no conviction of sin apart from seeing the glory of the Lord.

Those who imagine that morality must determine our destiny forget that morality can be put into operation by fear alone. The purpose of the law was partly to enforce morality through fear of punishment. Those who think that breaking the law after their conversion nullifies their salvation will be attaining to morality through fear of punishment (i.e., of losing their salvation). Hence they try to live moral lives. The mistake people make is that they call this morality "godliness." It is not that. Men can be moral and godless. Godliness will produce morality, let there be no doubt about that, but morality will never produce godliness. Godliness comes by conviction of sin, conviction of sin comes by seeing the glory of the Lord. Simon Peter saw the glory of the Lord, and he fell down at Jesus' feet, saying, "Depart from me; for I am a sinful man, O Lord" (Luke 5:8). The "blameless" Saul of Tarsus confessed that when he truly saw the righteousness of the law, "sin revived, and I died" (Romans 7:9).

Thus it is not godliness that drives us to live a straight life in order to prevent the loss of our salvation. Godliness is not selfishness. Godliness does not "seek its own" (cf. 1 Corinthians 13:5). If godliness is rewarded by salvation, then salvation is not free. Living a straight life in order to keep from invalidating our salvation is not godliness. It is morality that is produced exactly the same way the law produced it - through fear of punishment.

Godliness is living to the glory of the Lord when you realise it is done from the heart, out of gratitude. You cannot live in a godly manner for the glory of God as long as you have your own interest at stake. But when you see that God's justice has been truly satisfied by the death of Jesus and that righteousness is put to your account by faith alone, that is partly what is meant by seeing the glory of the Lord. The result: you have an opportunity to be truly godly. Godliness is never a valid option until we *see* that we are saved by the free grace of God. Before that it is something else morality, fear, carefulness, anxiety, walking a straight-line— but not godliness.

IT IS THE SPRINGBOARD FOR FELLOWSHIP WITH THE FATHER

In the general epistle of 1 John we are told of the possibility of fellowship with the Father (l John 1:3). We are told that it comes by walking in the light (John 1:7) and that truly doing so means that in us "is the love of God perfected" (1 John 2:5). John further tells us "there is no fear in love; but perfect love casteth out fear: because fear hath torment [has to do with punishment, NIV]. He that feareth is not made perfect in love" (1 John 4:18). It surely goes without saying that to the degree there is uncertainty about our final destiny, there is fear.

The possibility of perfect love should be sufficient basis for us to believe that once saved, always saved must be the certain knowledge for at least some.

Thus to the person in whom the love of God is perfected there is no fear, no torment, nothing to dread due to punishment. It is assumed that eternal salvation is assured. And yet that is not what that verse really means. For the assurance of our salvation was true without the love of God being perfected. That is why John wrote, "I write unto you, little children, because your sins are forgiven you for his name's sake" (1 John 2:12). He left them in no doubt they were saved in the first place. But what he did have some doubts about was whether or not his little children were enjoying what John liked to call fellowship with the Father or perfect love. Paul calls it "faith which worketh by love" and "walking in the Spirit" (Galatians 5:6,16,25). Jesus called it taking His yoke upon us and thus finding "rest unto your souls" (Matthew 11:29). As a matter of fact there are quite a number of names or descriptive biblical phrases for exactly the same thing that John calls "fellowship with the Father."

But as long as there is doubt about your eternal standing in God's grace, there will be an impediment to your having fellowship with the Father. For this fellowship with the Father cannot be truly enjoyed until you have the fullest and deepest respect for Him. You cannot have true respect for one who is basing your entire relationship on your own performance. If you feel you are constantly on trial, having to prove yourself, being analysed or feeling afraid that you will be cut off the moment you don't come up to standard, you don't really have respect for that person. You cannot be at ease with someone who is always testing your relationship by how well you are treating him (or her). If your view of

74

God is like that, do not be surprised if you do not have fellowship with Him. You don't really respect Him. But take the person who loves you all the time. Take that friend who knows all about you - and still likes you. Take that person who will not reject you no matter what secret fault you have. That is a real friend. You love to be with a person like that. What a relief to be away from those who are always suspicious of your motives, always putting your relationship to the test, always making you prove yourself. What a relief to be with someone who is totally accepting.

That is the way God is. Why? He has already been satisfied by the blood of Jesus. Oh, He was angry, yes indeed! we were "children of wrath" (Ephesians 2:3). But God has been perfectly and completely satisfied by His Son's performance. It was His Son who had to prove Himself. And He did it very well indeed - perfectly, without sin (2 Corinthians 5:21; Hebrews 4:15). As a consequence of His Son's performance, God accepts you as you are, warts and all. As for your weaknesses, you have at God's right hand the Lord Jesus who is touched by the feeling of your infirmities (He is not put off by your weaknesses, but feels them). This gives you the confidence to come boldly to the throne of grace to obtain mercy and find grace to help in time of need (Hebrews 4:15-16). Fellowship with God is possible because we are already in the family and cannot be disenfranchised.

It is knowing this that paves the way for fellowship with God. This fellowship means knowing God in this life at a depth that, alas, few Christians experience. There are more reasons than the impediment of not believing in eternal security that lie behind our lack of fellowship with the Father. I will come to that in a subsequent chapter. I am only trying to establish at this point that doubting our eternal salvation militates against this fellowship with God.

Take, for example, an insecure wife or husband who constantly doubts the other's love. If the marriage relationship has to be sustained by one or the other constantly trying to prove themselves, it makes for a very insecure marriage. It is disheartening to say to your wife or husband, "I love you" when the other says, "I wish I could believe that." If you have to keep proving it by words and deeds all the time and you still feel you aren't getting anywhere, you must see how frustrating the relationship will be until one simply takes the other's *word*. That is what God wants us to do. He wants us to believe Him—to take His word. But if, after all that He has done by sending His Son to die on a cross, He still finds us doubting His love, then fellowship with God will be a matter of tension rather than joy.

I know not a few Christians who have been converted for years and years but still question their assurance of eternal salvation. It is not because they don't believe in once saved, always saved but because they aren't really sure they have been *saved*. They don't have any trouble with the doctrine itself. They are only afraid that it doesn't apply to *them!* Such people don't realise they are in the very grip of Satan. They try to live in a godly manner, yes. But it gets them nowhere insofar as joy is concerned. Look at their faces. They have long faces, grim faces, sad faces. They have spent years hoping to have assurance of eternal salvation. They still haven't got it. Neither do they have fellowship with the Father. Oddly enough, some would try to claim fellowship with the Father before they would lay claim to being eternally saved! But people like that are often counter-productive - all because they don't take the simplicity of God's word to heart.

The purpose of this chapter is to demonstrate that believing in once saved, always saved is not an optional thing after all. Not that you have to believe it to be saved—no, I'm not saying that. But not to believe it means a lack of peace, no proper motivation for true godliness, and no foundation for fellowship with the Father.

I think that many of us have thought that believing once saved, always saved would be nice for some but not for all. Those who don't believe in it have really thought they were better off *not* to believe it. It is as though they don't trust themselves with such powerful teaching. They think that, were they to believe it, they would slip and do some things that are wrong (which they apparently want to do anyway). The truth is, all who do not believe this teaching are deprived. I do not deny that some have abused it. But the net result of this teaching will be that more will come into true godliness than ever before, more will have peace and joy than ever before, and more will be ready for and desirous of fellowship with the Father than ever before.

Once saved, always saved is a great thing to believe. And it *is* essential that we believe it - for our own good.

5

Justification By Faith

The greatest proof of once saved, always saved is the biblical teaching of justification by faith. I hope this won't seem unfair, but I have yet to meet the first person who had difficulty with once saved, always saved and who also had what seemed to me to be a clear understanding of what the Bible teaches about justification by faith. Had I wanted to begin by proving the theme of the book, I would have made this our first chapter.

This could well be the most thrilling chapter for the reader. For when it hits you that you are *justified* before God by faith in Jesus' blood, you might even be ashamed that you could have doubted your own salvation. But we have all done this. All of us have struggled with the very simplicity of the gospel. Time and again we end up saying it's just too good to be true. With that in mind the devil comes along and suggests it *is* too good to be true.

The best way to defeat the devil when he accuses us is to know exactly what the blood of Jesus does. We do not defeat the devil merely by "pleading the blood" if we don't understand why the blood of Jesus defeats the devil. The reason those we read of in Revelation overcame the devil "by the blood of the Lamb, and by the word of their testimony" (Revelation 12:11) was because they knew what the blood of Jesus did. Do we? That is the question. When we do, we are set.

When we understand Paul's language, "being now justified by his blood, we shall be saved from wrath through him" (Romans 5:9), we are in a position of safety, as it were, from doubting. I do not say we won't have doubts. But if ever there were a matter on which we must be clear it is the subject of this chapter. The devil always goes for the weakest link in our spiritual chain, and I can promise that if we are not strong on the present matter we remain an easy target for the devil. As long as we doubt our own justification, the devil will attack us at that very point. Why need he look elsewhere in order to defeat us?

You probably know that we are dealing with a doctrine that was rediscovered in the sixteenth century by Martin Luther (1483-1546). His discovery was utterly personal. He only wanted to know God for himself. He was not looking for ammunition to attack Rome. He was utterly loyal to Rome when he first discovered that faith alone satisfies the justice of God. It turned his life upside down. But he couldn't keep quiet about it, and it eventually turned the world itself upside down. Nothing has been the same since.

This chapter is not a defense of Luther. The doctrine of justification by faith is the foundation of the Reformation, but it is also the cornerstone of the Christian faith itself. So important is this teaching that if one's thinking on this matter is sound, it is highly unlikely that one will be given to any serious theological error.

That is a bold statement, but I think I can prove it. If one is sound on justification by faith it presupposes that one will be right on the nature and character of God, man, Jesus Christ, and salvation. These are the things that matter. it is not possible to be sound on justification by faith and have a faulty view of God, man, and Jesus Christ.

For example, it has always been interesting to me that so many of those who have a cloudy view of justification by faith are often attracted to a wrong Christology (what you believe about Jesus). What is a right Christology? You must believe that Jesus is God. You must believe that Jesus is man. He was God as though He were not man. He was man as though He were not God. *Jesus is the eternal, God in the flesh.* "In the beginning was the Word, and the Word was with God, and the Word was God. And the Word was made flesh, and dwelt among us" (John 1:1,14).

I have been amazed, even shocked, to discover how often those who do not believe what the Bible says about justification by faith are fascinated by false views about Jesus. I have discovered this melancholy fact among the most zealous young Christians as well as among the more sophisticated and learned theologians. I would challenge the reader to investigate the belief of anyone's doctrine of Jesus Christ who either has an unclear view of justification by faith or of once saved, always saved. Ask them: "Do you believe that Jesus is the eternal God in the flesh? I am not saying that all those who do not believe in once saved, always saved are heretics. Not at all. I am only saying that I have discovered an alarming number of people whose faulty conception of justifica-

81

tion by faith is matched by an inadequate view of the person of Jesus.

There is a network into which we must be tuned in order to avoid the pitfalls of theological error. These errors can be vast, overwhelming, and dangerous. I would therefore not hesitate to say that the doctrine of justification by faith is the best place to begin for the new Christian, even if he never intends to become a serious theologian. Knowing how we are saved is the key to solid Christian growth, balanced evangelism, and consistent biblical teaching.

It does not follow, however, that one must grasp *all* that may be known about justification by faith. For it is a teaching that is both simple and profound. It is so simple that the bare rudiments of it turned Luther's world upside down. It is so profound that an entire book twice the size of this one could treat the subject without needless repetition. Martin Luther himself did not perceive all of the implications of his own discovery. A year before he wrote his famous *95 Theses* (1517) he published his *Commentary on Romans*. This commentary is quite elementary compared to the way Luther's own teaching has been developed by his successors. One of the most fascinating discoveries about Luther is how comparatively little he himself knew when he wrote the 95 Theses. It is encouraging to know how God used a man who still had a lot to learn. Luther preached through Paul's Galatian's three different times and each successive time was clearer than the one before.

John Calvin (1509-1564) was much clearer on justification by faith than Luther. He had a generation to reflect upon Luther's discovery. Besides, Calvin did not inherit Luther's theological method. He had a different mind and was able to give a perspective on justification by faith that vindicated not only Luther but the doctrine once saved, always saved as well. Luther stressed what faith does; Calvin emphasising what Christ does. Luther built his case on faith alone (without works); Calvin put the weight on Christ's works alone. What I propose to do in this chapter is to give an outline not of what either Luther or Calvin taught but what the Bible teaches. But having said that, it would be foolish to deny that we are indebted not only to Luther and Calvin but to a host of learned and godly men since.

The most fundamental matter for us to grasp about justification by faith is that it refers to the way God sees us, not the way we see ourselves. Justification is "exterior" to ourselves. It lies utterly outside of us. It is wholly the way God sees us. That an interior change takes place in us due to regeneration (being born again) is not to be disputed. But justification properly belongs to the way God regards any man or woman who receives the gospel of His Son. In a word, we are regarded by God as though we possessed everything that Jesus did and suffered. Justification is forensic, that is, it is entirely a legal matter.

That may sound unexciting. But I urge you to work through these pages carefully. The reward is tremendous. What is legal may not sound very relevant. But once you reality we are talking about the way God will *judge* you - that matters. For God pronounces a particular judgment on those who trust His Son. What is that judgment? *They are declared righteous*. In short, they are regarded by the Father as though they possessed all that Christ did and suffered. God, the supreme judge, pronounces a sentence upon us. It is a sentence that will not be changed. It is irrevocable. That sentence is pronounced once a person has trusted Jesus Christ. The same sentence will be revealed on the Final Day. But the sentence itself was actually made long before, when one believed the promise.

All that the apostle Paul did in Romans and Galatians was to state what I have said above. Paul went into meticulous detail, of course. He pioneer's, as it were, a radical kind of thinking that no man thought he had heard before. And yet much of what he laboured to say simply showed it was *not* new. Paul insisted he was making no theological contributions, that Abraham and David had seen it long before.

For some of us who have difficulty understanding this teaching it may be helpful for the moment to separate justification from faith. The two are inseparable of course. But the breaks sometimes comes when each is examined separately. Justification is God's doing. It is His pronouncement. Only God can justify. Justification is God's prerogative alone. And yet He never justifies apart from faith. The Greek word for justification is *dikaiosune*. It may be translated "justification" or righteousness or "justice." Therefore, we might as easily be speaking of "righteousness by faith" or "justice by faith." For there is a justice *apart* from faith, namely, God's sentence of condemnation. Justice apart from faith is what we actually deserve. In a word, hell. Justice is giving one what is deserved. Grace is giving what is not deserved. This is why grace is "unmerited favour" Nobody deserves grace. All deserve justice, that is, justice based upon our own works. But the extraordinary thing, according to Paul, is that there is actually a justice by faith. It enables God to be just (true to Himself) and still give us an eternal reprieve.

The Bible says basically two things about God. First, that He is just. That means He must punish sin. You and I are sinners, therefore He must punish us. Second, the Bible says that God is merciful. That means He does not want to punish us. Here the obvious question emerges: How can God be just and merciful at the same time? Answer: He sent His Son - the God-man, Jesus Christ - into the world. When Jesus was on the cross, something happened that the naked eye could not see. No person watching the crucifixion knew about it. It was all behind the scenes. At some point on Good Friday - between twelve noon and three o'clock - the sins of the world were transferred to Jesus. "The Lord hath laid on him the iniquity of us all" (Isaiah 53:6). "He who knew no sin was made sin for us" (2 Corinthians 5:21). Sin is what caused Jesus' death. It was not the crucifixion - it was rather God Himself punishing Jesus. "The wages of sin is death" (Romans 6:23).

Jesus never sinned, so He ought not ever to have died. But why did He die? Because our sins were *transferred* to Him. "He bore our sins" (1 Peter 2:24). In a word, God can be merciful to us because He punished Jesus for our sins - that is how He can be just and merciful at the same time.

It is also how God can be just and save us - it is justice by faith. It is a declaration of God's righteousness (justice), says Paul, "that he might be just, and the justifier of him which believeth in Jesus" (Romans

3:26). It is God who pronounces us righteous, and yet He will not do that apart from faith.

That leads us to a rather complex but enlightening discussion on the matter of causes. There are actually two causes that lie behind justification by faith: the meritorious cause and the instrumental cause. The meritorious (or material) cause is Jesus Christ - alone. The instrumental cause is our faith - alone. The meritorious cause is the person and work of Jesus, not our words or our love, nor even our faith. If the meritorious cause were our faith, then faith would be a work after all. But faith is not the meritorious cause, it is the instrumental cause. The meritorious or material (what is physical or concrete) cause is Jesus. It is His life and death. When Paul said that we are "justified by his blood" and "saved by his life" (Romans 5:9-10), he meant what we (for the sake of clarification) are calling the meritorious cause. This is why Calvin called our faith an "instrument," a "kind of vessel," "something merely passive, bringing nothing of ours to the recovering of God's favour but receiving from Christ that which we lack" (Institutes, III:xi:7; xii:5).

Dr. Martyn Lloyd-Jones has put it like this:

> We must never say that it is our faith that saves us.... It is the Lord Jesus Christ who saves you. If you say that your faith saves you, your faith has become a work, and you have something to boast.... Faith does not save us; it is through faith we are saved. Faith is only the instrument, It is not the cause of justification.[1]

1. Martyn Lloyd-Jones, Romans, Vol 1: Atonement and Justification (Grand Rapids: Zondervan, n.d.) p. 47.

Therefore if you were to say that the apostle Paul says both - that Christ saves and that faith saves - you would be right. In Romans 5:9, Paul says we are "justified by his blood." In Romans 3:25, he says that God has set forth Christ to be a propitiation through "faith in his blood." The blood justifies. Faith justifies. Both are absolutely true and yet either would be ineffectual without the other. This is why Paul says that the righteousness of God is revealed "from faith to faith" (Romans 1:17). Here Paul's statement gives rise to what we have referred to as the meritorious cause - faith - and the instrumental cause - faith. How can faith be both? Because the "first" faith in Romans 1:17 is Christ's own faith (hence the meritorious cause). The "second" faith in Romans 1:17 is our own faith. His faith must be joined by our faith or there will be no justification. This is elaborated by the apostle when he again uses the expression "righteousness of God" but now tells us precisely what he means by the expression "faith to faith." "Even the righteousness of God which is by faith of Jesus Christ unto all and upon all *them that believe* (Romans 3:22).

The faith of Christ is therefore of no value until it is ratified by our faith. Galatians 2:16 says exactly the same thing: "Knowing that a man is not justified by the works of the law, but by the faith *of* Jesus Christ, even we have believed in Jesus Christ, *that we might be justified by the faith of Christ.*" If *pistis christou* (faith of Christ) means only faith in Christ, as some modern translations have led us to believe, then Paul is speaking redundantly in Romans 3:22 and Galatians 2:16. This is equally true of Galatians 2:20 and Galatians 3:22. For Jesus had a perfect faith, a concept that has not been taken seriously by some. When it was written, "I will put my trust in him" (Hebrews 2:13), the writer was affirming the very faith of Jesus. When Paul speaks of the faith of Jesus Christ he uses an all-embracing term that means the complete and utter righteousness of the very person of God's Son - His obedience, His death and even His intercessory work at God's right hand. "For if, when we were enemies, we were reconciled to God by the *death* of his son, much more, . . . we shall be saved by his *life*" (Romans 5:10). "It is Christ that died, yea rather, that is risen again, who is even at the right hand of God, who also maketh intercession for us" (Romans 8:34).

I hope we can see why the matter of causes is important. It clarifies so many verses in the New Testament. God's justification is revealed "from faith to faith" (Romans 1:17), the meritorious cause having to be joined by the instrumental cause. For if *we* do not believe, there is no justification. Had Paul said that the righteousness of God is revealed by the faith of Jesus Christ - full stop, then our faith is quite unnecessary. But all that Jesus was and did must be ratified by our faith. It is "from faith to faith." All that Christ did and suffered for the salvation of the human race is of *no value* until we believe. For although our faith is in no sense whatever a work, such faith must be present in our hearts or we will perish. To extract our own faith from God's justification is to sever the jugular vein of the Christian faith. He who believes shall be saved; he who does not believe shall be damned (Mark 16:16).

But we are not finished. One needs to see that the Bible speaks to two kinds of righteousness: a legal righteousness and a gospel righteousness. The legal

88

righteousness pertains to the law of Moses with all its works. The Mosaic law demands absolute and perfect righteousness in man (thought, word, and deed) - sixty seconds a minute, sixty minutes an hour, twenty-four hours a day every day of our lives. The man who wants to be saved by his works (the way all of us naturally feel) should be told that he has his work cut out for him. "Legal righteousness" is a hard road. To the one who opts for this route of righteousness there is inevitably bleakness and despair.

Such a man should take a look at Galatians 3:10: "For as many as are of the works of the law are under the curse: for it is written, Cursed is every one that *continueth not in all things* which are written in the book of the law to do them" (cf. Deuteronomy 27:26). For the route of legal righteousness is not accessible by good intentions. Sincerity is not enough. High motivation is not enough. Our best will not do. For it is utter and absolute righteousness that God demands of him who chooses to be saved by his works. How demoralising! But he can save himself a lot of time and trouble if he will take Paul's word for it: "Therefore by the deeds of the law there shall no flesh be justified in his sight" (Romans 3:20). Paul stated in the plainest language what one will find out sooner or later. Works do not - for they cannot - save us. Why? Because the standard of justice God requires is out of our reach.

But there is another kind of righteousness: gospel righteousness. Gospel means "good news." Perhaps you have never known before precisely why the gospel is good news. You should see why now. Jesus said, "I am not come to destroy the law, but to fulfil" (Matthew

5:17). That is exactly what Jesus did. He fulfilled it. He kept the law perfectly - from the cradle to the grave - and as a consequence of what He did the very same law that condemned us now pronounces us free.

The law must acquit us when we trust God's Son. For He was our substitute, the last Adam (1 Corinthians 15:45), doing perfectly everything that the first man failed to do. He lived without sin. His faith was without doubting. His obedience was consistent. As for His relationship to the Father, "I do always those things that please him" (John 8:29). When He died on the cross, He fulfilled the law by becoming "the Lamb of God, which taketh away the sin of the world" (John 1:29).

The good news, then, is that all that Jesus did and suffered is put to our account when we believe. "But of him are ye in Christ Jesus, who of God is made unto us wisdom, and righteousness, and sanctification, and redemption" (1 Corinthians 1:30).

That brings us to the term "imputation." That is in fact the key. Take away the word "imputation" or "imputed" from the doctrine of justification and all we are saying in this book crumbles to the ground. This matter is so important that we have not the slightest hope of once saved, always saved being true if imputation is withdrawn from the picture. It is the key. It means "put to the credit or account of." The idea did not originate with Paul. He stressed that point. All Paul did was to take advantage of the Old Testament word "imputed." He had two undoubted precedents to which he appealed for Old Testament support: Abraham and David.

One day Abraham, who had been a sun worshipper, walked out under the stars. It was obviously a clear night, for God said to Abraham, "Count the stars." Abraham began to count. He lost count. God said, "So shall thy seed be" (Genesis 15:5). What made God's word unbelievable (from the human standpoint) was that Abraham had no child at all and his wife Sarah was up in years. The most reasonable response (from a human standpoint) was for Abraham to say, "If that is true, I look forward to seeing it come to pass." But that is not what Abraham said. Rather "he believed the Lord." He actually *believed* what God told him! He *believed* that his seed would be as innumerable as the stars in the heavens. "Now faith is the substance of things hoped for, the evidence of things not seen" (Hebrews 11:1). Abraham had no evidence, but he had faith. Because he believed, God "counted it to him for righteousness" (Genesis 15:6).

That account of Abraham became the best illustration for Paul's doctrine of justification by faith. Moreover, because Abraham himself was not even circumcised at the time, Paul concluded that justification was by faith only. There were no works that justified Abraham, only faith. Therefore, Paul could say, "But to him that worketh not, but believeth on him that justifieth the ungodly, his faith is counted for righteousness" (Romans 4:5). In other words, God regarded Abraham as being just - righteous in His sight. How God judges us is what matters. Righteousness was *imputed* to Abraham. It was put to his credit. From that moment on, God regarded Abraham as a righteous man. Abraham's faith counted for righteousness.

Abraham was given righteousness because he believed God's promise with reference to his seed. According to Paul, we are given righteousness by believing God's promise with reference to His Son. Faith is believing God. It is believing His promise. It made no sense that Abraham would have a child. He and Sarah were both getting older and older. But Abraham believed the promise nonetheless.

Likewise, it makes no sense that we will be saved from God's wrath by the blood of Jesus. But we believe that promise. That counts for righteousness. That is Paul's doctrine.

He drew the same conclusion from a statement David made in Psalm 32:1-2: "Blessed is he whose transgression is forgiven, whose sin is covered. Blessed is the man unto whom the Lord imputeth not iniquity" (cf. Romans 4:6- 8). Whereas in the first case God imputed "righteousness" to Abraham, in the case of David it was an imputation of "no sin"—which comes to the same thing! In either case the matter of works does not enter the picture at all. (Keep in mind we are talking only about justification, not regeneration or sanctification.) Works are of no value whatever, insofar as God's declaring a man righteous is concerned.

It takes little imagination to see why Rome regarded this as dangerous teaching. Let us be fair and admit that it is in a sense dangerous teaching. Paul himself said as much. He called it a scandal. "But we preach Christ crucified, unto the Jews a stumbling block [Gr. *skandalon*], and unto the Greeks foolishness" (1 Corinthians 1:23). "Where is boasting then? It is excluded (Romans 3:27). But it is the heart of the gospel.

Sinners Jesus will receive:
Tell this word of grace to all
Who the heavenly pathway leave,
All who linger, all who fall;
This can bring them back again:
Christ receiveth sinful men.

James McGranahan

We may ask, then, just what kind of "righteousness" is put to our credit.? What precisely is "imputed" to us.? Our first answer must be that what God calls "righteousness" is righteous enough! If the most holy God declares me *righteous,* that is good enough for me. That alone makes me eternally secure. For what He in His sovereign pleasure has pronounced cannot be undone. His judgment is irrevocable.

But is there not a certain standard of righteousness that is imputed to us? Of course there is. It is the righteousness of the law. God made His will known through the law that He gave to Moses. That law has been variously understood as having three elements: moral (the Ten Commandments), civil (how people should govern themselves), and ceremonial (regulation of worship). We have seen however that Jesus fulfilled the law (Matthew 5:17). The law, therefore, pronounces us free. "For I through the law am dead to the law, that I might live unto God" (Galatians 2:19). It follows then that the righteousness that is imputed to us is the righteousness of the law. In other words, it is as though we had kept it perfectly.

But wait a minute. Who was it who kept this law perfectly? It was Jesus. How did He do it? By a perfect faith, a perfect obedience, a sinless life, an atoning death. It is at this point we can see partly why Paul came up with the matter of "imputation" in the first place. Paul used language in Romans 3:23-26 that required the word "impute" or its equivalent. If the Old Testament had not used the word, or even if such a word did not exist, Paul would have coined a new term! The key verse is Romans 3:26. For that is where Paul shows us precisely what it is that lay behind God's declaring us righteous: it is the faith of Jesus. "That he might be just, and the justifier of him which believeth in Jesus" (Gr. *ton ek pisteos Iesou*—"by the faith of Jesus").

It is to be regretted that most translations work too hard to make the Greek readable and consequently gloss over, if not underestimate, a most profound truth. Paul literally means that God is just in justifying us by the faith of Jesus. That is what lay behind our Lord's keeping of the law. A perfect faith produced a perfect obedience. Paul calls it obedience in Romans 5:19, whereas he calls it faith in Romans 3:26. It is the faith and obedience of Jesus, then, that lay behind Paul's use of "imputation" in Romans 4 (he uses the Greek word eight times). If I am justified by what Jesus did, it follows that what He did is put to my credit.

What is put to our credit, then, is the very righteousness of Jesus Christ. It is Jesus' own righteousness that is imputed to us. This means therefore that we have both an *unchangeable* righteousness and an *unimprovable* righteousness. The heart of once saved, always saved is the righteousness of our Lord Jesus Christ imputed to us. For once the righteousness of Jesus is put to my credit, I am, from that moment, judged by His faith, obedient and sinless. Paul could say, "I live by the faith of the Son of God" (Galatians 2:20). Paul rested his whole case upon the righteousness of Jesus.

It is a most humbling thing. Not only are we given an unchangeable standing before God, but our standing will be no better twenty years after our conversion than it was one minute after. For the righteousness of Jesus is unimprovable. The years of toil and faithfulness do not add the slightest bit to our standing. For once the righteousness of Jesus is put to our account, we are clothed with a robe that cannot be competed with in a thousand years.

> *Jesus, Thy blood and righteousness*
> *My beauty are, my glorious dress;*
> *Midst flaming worlds, in these arrayed,*
> *With joy Shall I lift up my head.*
>
> *This spotless robe the same appears*
> *When ruined nature sinks in years;*
> *No age can change its glorious hue,*
> *The robe of Christ is ever new.*
>
> Nicolaus Ludwig von Zinzendorf

The righteousness of Christ has sometimes been distinguished in two ways: His passive obedience (death on the cross) and His active obedience (sinless life). If only Christ's passive obedience is put to our account it follows that we must produce sufficient works on our own in order to be finally saved. That would mean that the death of Christ had covered our sins but that without Christ's active obedience imputed to us, we must, from the moment of our conversion, live a life worthy of eternal life to be saved in the end. Therefore, it becomes absolutely crucial to know whether the *active* obedience of Christ, as well as the passive obedience of Christ, is imputed to us.

How can we be sure that the active obedience of Christ is imputed to us? Paul answers that the righteousness of God is revealed "from faith to faith" (Romans 1:17), the faith of Jesus (meritorious cause) having been ratified by our faith (instrumental cause). The faith of Jesus encompasses *all* He did - not only His death but also His sinless life. "For if, when we were enemies, we were reconciled to God *by the death* of his Son, much more, being reconciled, we shall be saved *by his life*" (Romans 5:10). This is why Paul said, "Even the righteousness of God which is by faith of Jesus Christ unto all and upon all them that believe" (Romans 3:22). "Knowing that a man is not justified by the works of the law, but *by* the faith of Jesus Christ, even we have believed *in* Jesus Christ, that we might be justified by the faith of Christ, and not by the works of the law: for by the works of the law shall no flesh be justified" (Galatians 2:16). Had Christ not justified us by His faith the burden would be upon us to keep the works of the Law - which we could never do. Had our Lord not done *everything* for us, both by His sinless life as well as His atoning death, we could hardly call it "so great salvation" (Hebrews 2:3). But that which makes it such a wonderful salvation is that our Lord Jesus Christ, in and by Himself, did everything that is required of us. Simple trust in Him justifies us eternally before God. *All* that Jesus did and suffered is put to our account.

Indeed, it was the active obedience of Christ that guarantied our right to eternal life. For the Mosaic Law is summed up in this: "This do, and live" (Deuteronomy 4:1; 5:33). One must never forget that doing the law meant doing it perfectly. "Cursed be he that confirmeth not *all* the words of this law to do them" (Deuteronomy 27:26). It is the passive obedience of Christ that exempts us from eternal death and condemnation, but it is the active obedience of Christ that actually guarantees our right to eternal life. "This do, and live." Jesus *did* - and we live! He fulfilled the law *for* us. It is therefore not the "essential" righteousness of Christ (His deity) that is imputed to us; it is that which He *did* in fulfilling the law for us. We are saved utterly and completely by a substitute, Jesus Christ. He did everything for us by His life and by His death. As a consequence of faith in Jesus, we are given forgiveness of sins (through His death) and assurance of eternal life (by His life). When we believe, therefore, His imputed righteousness guarantees that we can never come into condemnation and that we will be judged by His own life. His very obedience is put to our credit. It is consequently an unimprovable righteousness that we are given. If I am a Christian for fifty years and have become increasingly godly with every passing year (which I hope would be true) I will still be judged by the same righteousness that was imputed to me when I first believed. It is humbling, but thrilling. For by this I know I can never be lost.

> *When from the dust of death I rise*
> *To claim my mansion in the skies,*
> *E'en then shall this be all my plea,*
> *Jesus hath lived, hath died for me!*
>   Nicolaus Ludwig von Zinzendorf

6

Sons Of God

There are so many ways by which one may arrive at the truth once saved, always saved. Having said that the doctrine of justification by faith is the greatest proof of this truth, I am now tempted to say that it is rather the New Testament teaching of the new birth. In the end I must leave it to the reader to decide if there is really such a thing as the "greatest" proof of this teaching.

What we will examine in this chapter might be called the "hidden" explanation for faith in Christ. In the previous chapter we discussed two "causes" of justification: the material (or meritorious) cause - Christ, and the instrumental cause - faith. If I were to keep the matter of causes open a bit longer, we could say that this chapter is a way of stating the "efficient" cause of justification by faith. It is sometimes called effectual calling. In other words, what lies behind faith in the first place ? Why is it that any of us have believed? How many of us have paused very long to examine carefully *why* it was that we have trusted Christ?

C. H. Spurgeon, the great preacher of the nineteenth century, once told this story. He said he was sitting in church and listening to a rather boring sermon. His mind began to wander. "Why is it that I am a Christian?," Spurgeon asked himself. "I am a Christian because I heard and believed the gospel," he thought. He continued, "But why did I believe?" He answered, "I believed because -." Then like a flash God opened the floodgates of heaven and Spurgeon concluded. "I saw that God was at the bottom of it all."

Spurgeon discovered the same truth that the apostle John stated in John 1:12-13: "But as many as received him, to them gave he power to become the *sons of God,* even to them that believe on his name: which were *born,* not of blood, nor of the will of the flesh, nor of the will of man, but of God." In a word, there is but one final explanation why you and I are Christians: We have been *born of God.* This alone makes us sons of God.

The Greek word that is translated "born" is *gennao.* It means "to beget," "generate," "produce,' or "bring forth." If one is born of God, then it is God who has done the bringing forth or producing. God produced us, He brought us to life. When we were "dead in sins," God "quickened us together with Christ" (Ephesians 2:5). Quickened means "made alive." The new birth is something God did. We didn't do it. God did.

A man by the name of Nicodemus, a ruler of the Jews, came to Jesus one night and was immediately confronted with this truth: "Except a man be born again, he cannot see the kingdom of God" (John 3:3). The word translated "again" comes from a Greek word that literally means "that which is from above." A man must therefore be born "from above." Nicodemus reacted to this statement by asking. "How can a man be born when he is old? Can he enter the second time into his mother's womb, and be born? (John 3:4). Jesus did not accommodate Nicodemus with the answer he might have wanted. Jesus merely said, "Except a man be born of water and of the Spirit, he cannot enter into the kingdom of God. That which is born of the flesh is flesh: and that which is born of the Spirit is spirit" (John 3:5-6). Our natural birth is "flesh," that is, our very creation has a natural explanation. Our parents gave us our natural birth. What was by "flesh" was by *procreation*. What was by the "Spirit" is *regeneration*. In other words, in either case it is brought about by God.

It is the Christian's responsibility to tell everybody about Jesus. What is more, it is our responsibility to *do all we can do* to bring people to faith in Christ. We are called to be God's "midwives," standing ready to bring a baby to birth. But there is one thing we *cannot* do - bring to birth where there was no impregnated seed! For only God can give life. Creation is God's act; regeneration is God's act. "I have planted, Apollos watered; but God gave the increase" (1 Corinthians 3:6). Only God can bring people to birth. "No man can come to me, except the Father which hath sent me draw him: and I will raise him up at the last day" (John 6:44).

It therefore follows that every person who has been born of God or "born again" is now a son (or daughter) of God. "Behold, what manner of love the Father hath bestowed upon us, that we should be called the sons of God: therefore the world knoweth us not, because it knew him not" (1 John 3:1). There is nothing more wonderful in the world than to be called a son of God. John says not only are we called that but such we are -

101

"now *are we* the sons of God" (1 John 3:2). John gave us the way by which we may know that we are sons of God. "Every one that doeth righteousness is born of him" (1 John 2:29).

It is extremely important that we examine the context of 1 John 2:29. When John says he that "doeth righteousness is born of him" he is not only referring to morality.

There are many "righteous" people in the world insofar as outward morality goes. There are Buddists and Hindus and Moslems that are outwardly clean as a pin. John's statement was placed in the context of his having referred to certain seducers of his "little children." "These things have I written unto you concerning them that seduce you" (1 John 2:26). Those seducers are now known as Gnostics. Gnosticism (taken from the Greek *gnosis*—knowledge) was the earliest threat, other than persecution, to come from outside the church. However, it became a threat from within. Gnostics "crept in unawares" (Jude 4). They wormed their way into the church, coming in, as it were, through the back door. They managed to get right into the membership of the church. They did great damage to the fellowship (see Jude 12-13; 2 Peter 2:12-22). They wanted to turn the Christian faith into an entirely new way of knowing God. They had "new" knowledge, a new way of knowing, one that they said would make Christianity better than ever.

But there was one thing that the Gnostics were unable to do - confess that *Jesus Christ was God in the flesh*. They could not bring themselves to confess that. So much of 1 John pertains to Christiology (what one believes about Jesus). When John said, "Whosoever denieth the Son, the same hath not the Father: but he that acknowledgeth the Son hath the Father also" (1 John 2:23), he was showing the contrast between these godless Gnostics and true believers. A Gnostic simply could not bring himself to say "Jesus is God."

As we saw earlier, the confession that Jesus is Lord (Romans 10:9) means that He is God. In 1 John 2:1 our Lord is called "Jesus Christ the righteous." Why could Jesus be called "righteous?" Because He was the eternal God made flesh. He was born of a virgin. He was the son of Mary, yes, but He was equally the Son of God. He had no earthly father (Matthew 1:20, Luke 1:3-35). Jesus could equally be called "righteous" because throughout His earthly life He never sinned (Hebrews 4:15; 2 Corinthians 5:21). The reason, then, that John spoke of "doing righteousness" (as that which one born of God does) is that it is the consequence of confessing that Jesus Christ is Messiah. That to John is "doing righteousness." Doing righteousness ultimately leads to godly living (1 John 3:6-9). But in the immediate context John shows that doing righteousness begins with confessing that Jesus is God. Such a confession is to be explained but one way: this person is "born of God." For confessing that Jesus is God was precisely what the Gnostics could not do.

We might pause to point out, moreover, that the particular Gnostics to whom John referred had not only wormed their way into the church but also made their exodus. "They went out from us, but they were not of us; for if they had been of us, they would no doubt have continued with us: but they went out, that they might be made manifest that they were not all of us" (l John 2:19). We might wish that every congregation could say as much. How many congregations have had to endure in their fellowship those who do not in their hearts believe that Jesus Christ is the eternal God? Such hypocrites create havoc in the fellowship of God's people. Often they either take over the congregation entirely (and that church becomes a Bible-denying, apostate church) or such a congregation eventually closes its doors. For reasons unknown to us John could happily report in the case of the church he was then involved with (probably at Ephesus) that they "went out from us." They never were saved, however. "For if they had been of us, they would no doubt have continued with us." Jude also avows that such hypocrites were never saved (Jude 4, 13,15).

I have taken the time to deal with the Gnostic problem for more than one reason: partly because these godless men were behind some of the more difficult passages of scripture (see 2 Peter 2:20-22) and also because we may further see the inseparable connection between regeneration and what we believe about Jesus Christ. "Doing righteousness" begins with confessing who Jesus is, and there is but one explanation for doing so - being born of God.

What is extraordinary, however, is that *we* should be called sons of God. Why is this extraordinary ? Because of what John says about Jesus. For Jesus is *the* Son of God, the "only begotten" Son of God. "For God so loved the world, that he gave his only begotten Son, that whosoever believeth in him should not perish, but have everlasting life" (John 3:16). Martin Luther called John

3:16 the Bible in a nutshell. It contains the truth of heaven, hell, faith, redemption, and the essential knowledge about Jesus Christ - all in one verse! Jesus is the only begotten Son of God - His "one and only" Son (NIV).

To put it another way: God only had one "natural" Son. God could never have more than one "natural" Son. Do you know why? It is because the true God *emptied Himself* when He became man. "Although He existed in the form of God, He did not regard equality with God a thing to be grasped, but emptied Himself, taking the form of a bond-servant, and being made in the likeness of men" (Philippians 2:6-7). When God became man, He did not deposit, as it were, 50 percent of Himself in Jesus as if to leave the other 50 percent for another "Jesus." Theologian Paul Tillich, in words reminiscent of ancient Gnosticism, would not rule out the possibility of there being "another" Christ than Jesus of Nazareth at some point in time. But there could *never* be another. Why? Because in Jesus "dwelleth *all* the fullness of the Godhead bodily" (Colossians 2:9; "all the fullness of the Deity lives in bodily form" NIV). Jesus was 100 percent man. Jesus was 100 percent God.

And yet *we* are sons of God! How can this be? Answer: God brought us to birth. Jesus always was. He was not created, He was Creator. "In the beginning was the Word, and the Word was with God, and the Word was God . . . all things were made by him; and without him was not anything made that was made" (John 1:1-3). Jesus Christ never had a beginning. "For by *him* were all things created, that are in heaven, and that are in earth, visible and invisible, whether they be thrones, or dominions, or principalities, or powers: all things were created by *him,* and for *him:* and *he is* before all things, and by *him* all things considered' (Colossians 1:16-17). But *we* have had a beginning. We are the object of God's creation. Moreover, everyone that "doeth righteousness is born of God" (1 John 2:29). God has brought us to a second birth, a birth that has its origin "above." We are born into God's family. "Therefore if any man be in Christ, he is a new creature [creation]: old things are passed away; behold, all things are become new" (2 Corinthians 5:17). This is Paul's language for the new birth.

Does the new birth in and of itself guarantee that we will never be lost? Yes. Because our new creation is engendered by God's own Spirit who, according to Jesus, would abide "for ever" (John 14:16). The new life in us is God Himself. God cannot die. Whether this new life is called God's Spirit (1 Corinthians 3:16) or His "seed" (1 John 3:9), we are talking about the life of God Himself. It is the life of God in the soul of man. Moreover, this life was given to us "not according to our works" (2 Timothy 1:9) and it is unthinkable that such life would be turned over to us, as if we were obligated to "keep ourselves alive." Even at the purely natural (or physical) level, the life we have is of God. He determined the date of our birth, the choice of our parents and the colour of our eyes. "In him we live, and move, and have our being" (Acts 17:28). Likewise, at the spiritual level it is God who engendered us. "Being confident of this very thing, that he which hath begun a good work in you will perform it until the day of Jesus Christ"

(Philippians 1:6). "I give unto them eternal life; and *they shall never perish*, neither shall any man pluck them out of my hand" (John 10:28).

I think it would be helpful if we took a slightly closer look at this word regeneration, the best term for the new birth. Regeneration is an internal, sovereign work of the Holy Spirit. "The wind bloweth where it listeth, and thou hearest the sound thereof, but canst not tell whence it cometh, and whither it goeth: so is every one that is born of the Spirit" (John 3:8). Like the wind, nobody can manipulate or control the Holy Spirit. Moreover, it does not follow that regeneration is always a conscious experience at first. It may surprise you that I say this. But it is true. Regeneration is the hidden work of the Holy Spirit, that is, it almost always begins unconsciously. We cannot be sure precisely when it began. Regeneration, being born again, goes before faith. You may know when you first consciously began to believe, but God's secret work was in operation before then. As Augustus Toplady put it, "You may know the sun is up, although you were not awake when it arose." Regeneration produces faith. You could not have believed had not the Holy Spirit been at work before, even if it was a split second before!

It is not necessary to grasp this at first. We are into some rather heavy stuff. But I felt I had to deal with this for the one whose mind will not stop with the ABCs.

When we are "babes in Christ," we are not conscious of many of the sovereign ways of God. We discover more as we grow older in Christ. As children do not tend to appreciate their own parents until they get older, so it is with us as we grow in grace and knowledge (2 Peter

3:18). When we first believe and confess Jesus Christ as Lord, it often seems as though it is our own work. Many of us die hard on this matter. We don't like to concede that what we did, often with great pain and agony, was nothing but God working in us - that God (as Spurgeon put it) was "at the bottom of it all." But the truth is, God was at work before we acknowledged His Son. As conception precedes birth by some nine months, so the secret work of the Spirit may precede saving faith by many months. The second verse of John Newton's immortal hymn "Amazing Grace" states it well:

> 'Twas grace that taught my heart to fear,
> And grace my fears relieved;
> How precious did that grace appear
> The hour I first believed!

What made John Newton's heart to fear was in fact regeneration. God was at work even then. It almost always begins as an unconscious work.

Regeneration must also be seen as an *internal* work. It is God's life in us, His work going on right inside of us. Paul calls it "the law of the Spirit of life" which emancipates us from the law of sin and death (Romans 8:2). Paul chose to describe regeneration in his letter to the Romans after his discussion on justification. He waited until chapter eight to show the details of the hidden explanation for the faith which justifies. Faith is made possible by the Spirit in us. This is what changes one's life. Regeneration therefore is also what makes sanctification possible. For if there were no new life in us, there would be no possibility of the "righteousness of the law" being "fulfilled in us" (Romans 8:4). We shall return to the matter of sanctification later in this book.

We come now to what I would regard as perhaps the most sublime truth of all. This is possibly the most thrilling, the most dazzling disclosure this book has yet treated. I would also regard it as another incontrovertible fact of our unconditional security as sons of God: adoption.

There are thus two ways in which the matter of our sonship is described in the New Testament the new birth and adoption. The new birth, as we have seen, is God's internal act by which we are born into His family. Adoption is His external act by which we are chosen as members of His family.

We must return again to the person of Jesus Christ. We have seen that He is the eternal - indeed unique - Son of God. And yet we are sons of God! How is this possible? We have been adopted by the Father. God had only one "natural" Son. He has many adopted sons. Jesus is called the "firstborn among many brethren" (Romans 8:29). Like justification, adoption is exterior to us. In justification we are made righteous; in adoption we are made sons. Furthermore, whereas Jesus is the *eternal* Son of God, having been with the Father from all eternity, adoption brings us into the family at a certain *time*. Although God planned our adoption from the foundation of the world, the witness of our adoption comes in time, at some point after our natural birth. As God always had a Son but waited until "the fullness of the time was come" before He "sent forth his Son" (Galatians 4:4), so also has our adoption been known from the foundation of the world but the witness of it awaits God's own timing.

There is therefore a distinction to be made between adoption and the witness of our adoption. Adoption itself is God's secret act behind the scene, as it were; the witness of adoption is God's revealed act, in our hearts. "And because ye are sons, God hath sent forth the Spirit of his Son into your hearts, crying, Abba, Father" (Galatians 4:6). The witness of our adoption, then, is the Holy Spirit. It is the *conscious* work of the Spirit. I said earlier that regeneration is an unconscious work because we don't always know precisely when God began to work in us. But there comes a time when the Holy Spirit is known to us in a real and wonderful way. The same regeneration that makes sanctification possible is what makes the knowledge of our adoption possible.

For the reader who enjoys thinking in a rather methodical way, let me put it like this. What is sometimes called *ordo salutis* (order of salvation) has relevance here. Which comes first, the chicken or the egg? One may say it does not matter. Perhaps it is not necessary to know this sort of thing in depth, but it is nonetheless helpful to see how the Spirit operates in us. Paul spent a lot of time on this and we are impoverished by not trying to come to grips with this matter. To simplify, the order is this: regeneration, faith, the witness of the Holy Spirit. There are some who may insist that all three happen at the same time. I would not disagree, for God can do anything. With God all things are possible. But both Scripture and Christian experience will bear out that there is generally an order, a plan which God has unfolded. Regeneration precedes faith and faith pre-

110

cedes the witness of the Spirit. Regeneration gave birth to faith; faith gives birth to the witness of the Spirit.

I think it is important to see the order, if only because some Christians may get discouraged if the witness of the Spirit is not so prominent. It would be a grave mistake if we were to claim that those who do not feel the witness of the Spirit do not have faith (and therefore have not been regenerated or born again). In Galatians 4:6 Paul stated that the Spirit is sent forth "because ye *are* sons." In other words, their sonship was already guaranteed. It is not the Spirit's coming in this manner that *made* them sons - they already were sons. All the Spirit did was to testify to this fact.

Speaking personally, what happened to me on October 31, 1955 did not make me a Christian. I became a Christian on Easter Sunday morning in 1942. I am convinced that I was justified by faith on that very day. Regeneration was what prompted me to approach my parents in tears that morning, an hour before we went to church. I actually went to them. Weeping and with deep concern I said to them. "I want to become a Christian. I want to receive Jesus." I am thankful that they had the perception to accept my request seriously. They might have said to themselves, "He's too young to know what this is all about." Or they might have said to me, "Wait until you are a bit older." But they received me at once and knelt with me beside their bed. I got up from my knees *saved!* Over the next few years I grew in grace. I must also add that I had some happy times with the Lord. But something happened to me on October 31, 1955, which was quite different. It was an undoubted assurance of my being chosen into the family of God.

I would not want the reader to judge his or her own spiritual state by my or anyone else's particular experience. If you feel that regeneration, faith and the witness of your adoption happened at the same time, I think that is absolutely fine. I have no quarrel with you. Furthermore, if you have not had the equivalent of an experience like mine on October 31, 1955, it means neither that you are not saved nor that you do not have the Holy Spirit dwelling in you. But what I would have thought to be important is this: Most people that I have talked with (in my twenty-eight years of being in the ministry) did not have an extraordinary kind of assurance when they first believed in Christ. Such came later.

But before we say more about the witness of our adoption let us talk about adoption itself. What does it mean? It means that all of us are Jesus' brothers and sisters. That's right! That is what we are. Jesus is our big brother, our elder brother. We have in common the same heavenly Father. Jesus alone is the Father's only "natural" Son. The rest of us are adopted. Jesus is the "natural" Son. We have been grafted into the family.

But now for the most wonderful thing of all: we are joint heirs with Jesus. "The Spirit himself beareth witness with our spirit, that we are the children of God: and if children, then heirs; heirs of God, and *joint-heirs with Christ;* if so be that we suffer with him, that we may be also glorified together" (Romans 8:16-17). All that Jesus was to inherit is ours. Nothing could stop Him from obtaining His inheritance; nothing can therefore stop us.

Now let me pose this question: What would you say the possibilities are that-Jesus could be disinherited by

His Father? Do you really think that there is any chance that Jesus could be disenfranchised? Can Jesus be dislodged from the Godhead, from the Trinity?

You know the answer to that! But we are joint heirs with Jesus. There is no more possibility that we can be dislodged from the family of God than that Jesus could be disenfranchised by His Father. Our security is the same. There is absolutely no difference. For we are in Christ:

> Blessed be the God and Father of our Lord Jesus Christ, who hath blessed us with all spiritual blessings in heavenly places in Christ: according as he hath chosen us *in him* before the foundation of the world, that we should be holy and without blame before him in love: having predestinated us unto the adoption of children *by Jesus Christ to himself*, according to the good pleasure of his will, to the praise of the glory of his grace, wherein he hath made us accepted *in the beloved*. (Ephesians 1:3-6)

Adoption is thus the irrevocable guarantee that all that Jesus was to inherit we will too. Now that He has been raised from the dead and made to sit at the right hand of God, we know that we too will follow in His steps. Nothing can stop that. Nothing. "Who shall separate us from the love of Christ?" (Romans 8:35). "For I am persuaded, that neither death, nor life, nor angels, nor principalities, nor powers, nor things present, nor things to come, not height, nor depth, nor any other creature, shall be able to separate us from the love of God, which is in Christ Jesus our Lord" (Romans 8:38-39).

A few years ago, my wife and I witnessed the adoption of a child in a Fort Lauderdale, Florida, courtroom. We listened to the judge as he spoke to the adopting parents in gravest tones. "Before I sign my name to this document," he warned them, "I need to know that you realize what you are about to do." In a room of sobering silence in which you could hear a pin drop, that judge looked each parent straight in the eye and said, "If I sign my name to this document, there is no court in the United States that will overturn this order. If I sign my name to this document, it means that this child is yours, legally yours, as though he were your natural son. There is no guarantee how he will turn out. He may disappoint you. He may turn to drugs as a teenager. He may develop a serious illness and you will be responsible to care for him. If I sign my name to this document, that means this child is yours from this day forward. He is protected by the laws of this state. You cannot turn him back once I sign my name to this document. Do you understand this?"

Those parents did not hesitate to answer. "We understand," they responded. "Then is it your will that you become the parents of this child?" the judge asked. "It is," they replied. The judge signed the order. In what I thought was a rather unusual gesture, he got off his seat and walked round to the two parents and congratulated them. Every eye was filled with tears. The judge then revealed that he too had an adopted child.

"Behold, what manner of love the Father hath bestowed upon us, that we should be called the sons of God" (1 John 3:1). This is what we are, by irrevocable adoption. The family of God is comprised of adopted children. It is a company so vast that John considered it a "great multitude, which no man could number" (Revelation 7:9). Not one of them will be lost. Not one! Should one stray from the fold, God will go to great pains to bring that one back. "What man of you, having a hundred sheep, if he lose one of them, doth not leave the ninety and nine in the wilderness, and go after that which is lost, until he find it? And when he hath found it, he layeth it on his shoulders, rejoicing" (Luke 15:4-5).

A great benefit of being God's adopted children is found in Romans 8:28: "And we know that all things work together for good to them that love God, to them who are the called according to his purpose." This is God's absolute promise to everyone in the family: All things work together for good. This means the things that had not been good. Why say that? Because if they were already good, they would have no need to "work together for good." It is what is bad that God fits into a pattern for good. My sins, my sorrows. God promises me that "all things work together for good." It is what *He* does. If I try to make things work together for good, things get worse. It is when I turn everything over to God and say, "Its too much for me," that God takes over. "Let me handle it, He promises. Romans 8:28 is God's responsibility not mine.

So with my eternal salvation: "Who shall lay anything to the charge of God's elect? It is *God that Justifieth* Who is he that condemneth? It is *Christ that died*" (Romans 8:33-34). It is God's responsibility, not mine. "He which hath begun a good work in you will perform it until the day of Jesus Christ" (Phil. 1:6).

That is what adoption means. The *witness* of our adoption is nothing but the Spirit's testimony that we ourselves *have been adopted* into the family of God. It is the Spirit's witness to what has already been true. It began with regeneration and faith, but the Spirit impresses powerfully on the soul how real all this is. "For God hath not given us the spirit of fear; but of power, and of love, and of a sound mind" (2 Timothy 1:1). "For ye have not received the spirit of bondage again to fear; but ye have received the Spirit of adoption, whereby we cry Abba, Father" (Romans 8:15). The ancient word *abba* was the equivalent of our term "daddy"

We may ask, how is this witness of the Spirit known? There is the *mediate* witness and the *immediate* witness. The mediate witness is the Word of God, the Bible. We may read it, believe it, and thereby *conclude* from it that we are children of God. The mediate witness always leads to a conclusion - "therefore." The old Puritans called it the "practical syllogism." A major premise is followed by a minor premise which leads to a certain conclusion.

For example, "All who trust Christ are saved" (major premise); "I have trusted Christ" (minor premise); "Therefore I am saved" (conclusion). This is a real, firm, and infallible witness. It is *mediated* by the Word of God. It is the essence of faith. No child of God can be without it. For anyone *knows* whether or not his trust is in Christ alone.

If it is, he may conclude that he has been adopted into the family, "sealed unto the day of redemption:' as Paul put it (Ephesians 4:30) - a comment that only makes sense if our adoption is irrevocable.

But there is also the immediate witness of the Spirit. This however does not make a person "more" saved or "more" regenerated or "more" justified. This is not possible. Once saved, always saved. If one has the *mediate* witness one is eternally saved. One is not saved by the immediate witness; one is saved by the mediate witness - simple trust in the general promise of God.

The immediate witness of the Spirit is the Spirit's own witness, that is, the witness of the very Spirit Himself. Regeneration, as we have seen, is an unconscious work. Faith itself, however, is conscious. We know whether or not our trust is in Christ. But even in faith the conclusion is ours, that is we conclude that we are children of God by virtue of our own faith. Therefore, although faith itself is conscious, because we know we have believed, it does not follow that we have the immediate witness of the Spirit. For the immediate witness of the Spirit is direct it speaks directly to the heart, as if by-passing the "practical syllogism." The immediate witness of the Spirit renders the practical syllogism unnecessary, for the Spirit Himself testifies without our having to go through a major premise, a minor premise and conclusion. The Spirit simply does it all for us.

The immediate witness of the Spirit need not be present for true faith to be present. No one should hastily conclude, "I am not saved" if he does not have this immediate witness. Faith saves. Trusting Christ saves. Nothing more. The immediate witness is, as Dr. Lloyd-Jones put it, the "highest form of assurance." It happened to D. L. Moody years after he was a Christian. He was walking down a street in Brooklyn, New York.

117

Suddenly and unexpectedly he felt a surge of the Holy Spirit's power come upon him. The witness was so strong he thought he was going to die! He literally begged God to have mercy on him and stop it, lest he die right there on the street.

D. L. Moody was saved before that day, however. I was saved before October 31, 1955. Many Christians have testified to a similar experience. But it did not have the slightest thing to do with their getting to heaven. It only gave them greater assurance that they were going to heaven.

The immediate witness of the Spirit is another evidence of once saved, always saved, however. In what way? There could never be an immediate witness to adoption if an irrevocable adoption was not already there. The very possibility of an "earnest of the Spirit" (2 Corinthians 1:22) is proof enough of once saved, always saved. How else could God assure anybody of such if heaven were not an irrevocable gift to the believer? The very possibility, then, of the immediate witness of the Spirit is one more piece of evidence that those whom God has called will be justified. Moreover, "whom he justified, them he also glorified" (Romans 8:30).

The promise of being sons of God, then, assures us that we have an absolute security in the family of God. God will no more disinherit any of His own than He would reject His one and only Son. I am as secure as Jesus Himself. God wants me to know that. And never doubt it.

7

Sanctification And The Kingdom Of God

In the introduction to this book I referred to my own background and the manner in which I came to understand the doctrine once saved, always saved. At first, I honestly thought I had discovered something new. I naively imagined that I was on to a truth that had lain hidden since the days of the apostle Paul. The reason was mainly this: Although I knew that I myself was eternally saved, thus paying homage to the doctrine of "eternal security" I had long held to be wrong, I wasn't so sure that all Christians had the same security. In other words, I thought at first that only a few Christians could know what I knew.

I think I was partly right. The experience that brought me to embrace this teaching came more than twenty-eight years ago. I have had a lot of time to think about what happened to me and I have had a lot of time to search the Scriptures. I have concluded that not all Christians are given the kind of experience I had on October 31, 1955. In this sense not all have the same measure of assurance. Although such an experience is most certainly *available* to all Christians, not all seek the

Lord as earnestly as they might. Consequently, they do not find the reality of God's presence that could be their own inheritance.

But I was quite wrong in thinking that not all Christians had the same security. I was unable to make a critical distinction between the security that all Christians have and the degree of assurance of the same security. What happened to me on October 31, 1955 in actual fact did not make me more secure in Christ than I had been since I prayed to receive Christ in my parents' bedroom on Easter Sunday morning 1942. It could not make me "more saved" than I had always been. I felt "more saved," yes. Jesus was so real to me. I can state with utter candour that for several days the person of Jesus was more real to me than my room-mates in college or any particular individual. There was a time (it did not last indefinitely) during which Jesus was more real to me than my own existence. I cannot exaggerate this. And yet it would be wrong to say that the same experience made me any surer of heaven than I had been for many years before.

In other words, I was no more regenerate (born again); I was no more justified (righteous in God's sight); I was no more forgiven for my sins than I was on Easter Sunday morning 1942. But the *awareness* of these truths was heightened a hundred times. They were so real to me. This is why I knew I was eternally saved, no matter what I did in ensuing years. I have not wavered on that conviction since that memorable day. What I have had to reassess is the assumption that the security I had was exclusive to me (or Christians who may have had a similar experience). I now believe that *all* who in their *hearts* believe that Jesus died on the cross for their sins and that He rose from the dead (and confess this) are as secure as I ever was.

My reason for telling the above is this: my own background has influenced my approach to the Scriptures. I have had to work overtime in ridding myself of a lot of the excess baggage I inherited. It has not been easy. I have known the swinging of the pendulum from one extreme to the other, from a categorical rejection of much of what I had been taught to a benign adulation of some of the preachers I admired as I grew up. I do not want to be so naive now as to imagine I am rid of all excess baggage and that I have at long last gotten it right in all areas. I am still growing. What I do suspect is that God in His providence has brought me to consider various aspects of doctrine that many (who do not know the pain of changing their views) have not had the need to consider. It is for this reason I have wondered if perhaps I might have a small contribution to make in the theological realm of what is called "saving faith."

Because of my background I possibly know better than many the various Scriptures that are used to disprove the doctrine of once saved, always saved. Those who have been brought up to believe this teaching generally tend to ignore certain biblical passages. They merely stick to their guns by quoting John 10:28 or Romans 8:35. What many people have failed to do is to begin by looking carefully at Hebrews 6:4-6; 10:26; and Galatians 5:19-21.

I am quite certain that all I am saying in this chapter has been said before. In my travels around Britain I occasionally have a book shown to me written by someone who has said in certain statements what I myself have been holding to for a good number of years. I am greatly encouraged when this happens. I take no pleasure in trying to say something that is regarded by some as innovative. Like Calvin, who quoted Augustine every time he could do so, I much prefer to quote some respected authority who said it first. On the other hand, the trouble with quoting someone is that the issue takes off on a tangent in which academics debate the question of whether or not one correctly interpreted such a particular authority. At the end of the day nobody seems to know for sure. I, therefore, am not going to quote many people to substantiate the position taken in this book - I am sticking to the Bible. This is not an academic book in any case. As I stated earlier, I only want to encourage believers who desperately want to believe they are eternally secure in Christ but are afraid there is still a possibility they could be lost in the end.

That is why I write this chapter. I do not know of a single verse in the Bible that militates against the doctrine once saved, always saved. But I know a good number of passages that speak of "falling away" being "rejected," and not "inheriting the kingdom of God." It would only discourage the reader if we should ignore *any* passage in the Bible that has been seen as threatening to our teaching. I have consciously sought to deal with every single "doubtful" verse.

That which stands out with striking boldness in the New Testament is the unchanging nature of salvation and the dynamic nature of our inheritance in the kingdom of God. In other words, salvation is unchangeable but our inheritance in the kingdom of God is not unchangeable. Once *saved,* always saved, but our *inheritance* in God's kingdom may change considerably. It is surprising how little this has been emphasised. The problem instead has been a polarisation between Calvinists (those who believe that a regenerated person cannot ever lose his salvation) and Arminians (those who believe that disobedience may forfeit one's salvation). The Calvinists have tended to be ambiguous on passages like 1 Corinthians 6:9-10, while Arminians think that one's inheritance in the kingdom of God and being saved rise or fall together. In other words, both Arminians and Calvinists generally have tended to regard one's inheritance in the kingdom of God and having salvation as quite the same thing.

I believe that the Arminians and many Calvinists have missed an important teaching with regard to salvation and the kingdom of God. Arminians have argued that the loss of an "inheritance" in God's kingdom obviously means that such a person no longer has salvation. After all, Paul says that he who does the works of the flesh "shall not inherit the kingdom of God" (Galatians 5:21). No one who gives in to sexual sin or covetousness "hath any inheritance in the kingdom of Christ and of God" (Ephesians 5:5).

Verses like these are conclusive for the Arminian, especially when he hears the Calvinist explanation for these verses. The Calvinist dismisses the whole matter by saying that saved people do not "practice" or "continue" in such wickedness for those who do merely show they were not saved in the first place. Some Calvinists grant that a saved person may indulge in such sinfulness for a while, but not indefinitely. This is nice in theory. But when a professing Christian candidly says, "I just can't stop this sin at the moment," the Arminian must conclude that such a person is no longer a Christian. The traditional Calvinist has to say either, "This person was never saved," or "There is no reason at the moment to believe this person is saved." The Calvinist with a pastoral heart may secretly hope such a person is a Christian, but he would have a stronger basis of hope should he take another look at Galatians 5:21, Ephesians 5:3-5, and 1 Corinthians 6:9-10, for a start.

What I have sought to do is to take these Scriptures seriously (if not literally) without trying to uphold a theological position I felt I must defend. Perhaps the greatest curse on theology is the defensiveness that leads to entrenchment. So many of us get entrenched in a position we may not believe in our hearts but think we must nonetheless defend. Astonishingly little theological advancement has been made over the years as a consequence. I am no less vulnerable to being entrenched, for here I am presenting a book which takes a fairly strong view. I would ask, though, the reader's indulgence by following me into a vast, beautiful garden. It is a garden lush with lovely trees and ripe fruit. Not all the trees are the same, although from a distance they may look the same.

The kingdom of God is a prominent New Testament theme which, from a distance, might appear to denote the same thing each time the expression is used. Sometimes the kingdom of God and salvation do mean essentially the same thing, as in John 3:3: "Except a man be born again, he cannot see the kingdom of God." By "see the kingdom" Jesus apparently meant "enter" it, for when He restated the same point a moment later He said that unless a man be born of water and of the Spirit "he cannot enter into the kingdom of God" (John 3:5). Obviously Jesus was saying that if anyone is born again he is *in* the kingdom of God, the new birth alone having accomplished that. We may safely conclude that the person who has been "born again" has been saved and therefore translated "into the kingdom of his dear Son" (Colossians 1:13). Having salvation and being in the kingdom of God may thus mean essentially the same thing.

But not always. That is why Jesus gave so many parables of the kingdom of heaven. Whatever else the parables do, they represent various descriptions and applications of what Jesus called the kingdom of heaven. The kingdom of heaven and the kingdom of God are the same thing (cf. Matthew 4:17; Mark 1:15). The parables of Jesus sometimes show the mixture of saved and lost people within the confines of the "visible" kingdom. By "visible" kingdom I mean what is often called the visible church, that is, all people who *profess* to be Christians, whether or not they truly are. Sometimes, however, the parables of Jesus demonstrate the mixture of strong and not so strong people who are nonetheless Christians. Whatever the analogy Jesus sought to put forward, it was always within the framework of what He called the "kingdom of heaven." The parables are intended to represent the conditions we are likely to encounter in the church and in living the Christian life.

In Antioch Paul and Barnabas exhorted the disciples "to continue in the faith, and that we must through much tribulation enter into the kingdom of God" (Acts 14:22).

This would be a very strange comment indeed if the kingdom of God and having salvation were always the same thing. For if the kingdom of God and salvation were always the same thing, it would only follow from Acts 14:22 that first, continuance in the faith comes *before* being saved; and second, salvation comes by *suffering* ("tribulation"); and third, the hearers of Paul and Barnabas, though called "disciples," were *not saved yet*. In other words, if salvation and the kingdom of God were always synonymous (and rise or fall together), then Acts 14:22 militates against all that Paul taught regarding justification (in Romans 3 and 4) and adoption (in Romans 8 and Galatians 4).

But if someone counters that the kingdom of God in Acts 14:22 merely means heaven it follows that: first, one only gets to heaven by tribulation, and second, there is no way of knowing one will make it to heaven until one is there. This refutes the Pauline doctrine of assurance and would make nonsense of Hebrews 9:12: "Neither by the blood of goats and calves, but by his own blood he entered in once into the holy place, having obtained eternal redemption for us."

But is Acts 14:22 an odd exception? I think not. If anything the references to the kingdom of God (there are no fewer than 150 explicit references to it in the New Testament) are less concerned to demonstrate once saved, always saved than they are other truths. In fact the Pauline usage of the phrase "kingdom of God" almost always refers to faithfulness, obedience, or reward ("inheritance"). We shall see below what this reward is, but nothing is clearer to me than this: One can be saved but not necessarily obtain a "reward of inheritance"

(Colossians 3:24) in the kingdom of God. "Know ye not that the *unrighteous* shall not inherit the kingdom of God ? Be not deceived: neither fornicators, nor idolaters, nor adulterers, nor effeminate, nor abusers of themselves with mankind, nor thieves, nor covetous, nor drunkards, nor revilers, nor extortioners, shall inherit the kingdom of God. And such *were some of you*: but ye are washed, but ye are sanctified, but ye are justified in the name of the Lord Jesus, and by the Spirit of our God" (1 Corinthians 6:9-11).

When Paul says "such were some of you," he was not referring merely to their pre-conversion past but to the way "some" of them had been behaving since they had been saved. If he had referred only to their pre-conversion past, it means that only "some" of them were these things before they were saved (when in fact all men could be described by some of these categories before conversion). What was Paul so concerned about with these Corinthians.? It was precisely that some of them were not living the godly lives that Paul had taught them to live. But did Paul threaten them by taking away the hope of their salvation.? Not at all. "But ye are washed, but ye are sanctified, but ye are justified." Never once did he scold them by saying, "The trouble with you people is you're just not saved." That would be some people's remedy nowadays. Some think the only way to get a backslider straightened out is to moralise and say to him, "You must not be saved after all."

That was not Paul's method because that was not his theology. One need but read 1 Corinthians to see that Paul was most unhappy with the way many of them were living. He was very upset with them. But if one thinks that Paul went to Corinth to preach morality alone, and that this is all he meant in 1 Corinthians 6:9, then all he said about knowing nothing among them "save Jesus Christ, and him crucified" (1 Corinthians 2:2) cannot really be taken seriously. Statements such as "the unrighteous shall not inherit the kingdom of God" are indeed understood by some sincere Christians to mean that "we get to heaven by being good." Is *that* what Paul meant? How could this be true when he had previously said, "But of him are ye in Christ Jesus, who of God is made unto us wisdom, and righteousness, and sanctification, and redemption" (1 Corinthians 1:30)?

What amazes me is how Paul *began* 1 Corinthians with such profound statements about salvation and justification when he knew he was addressing a number of Christians who had seriously abused that very gospel. The conduct of many of these Corinthians would be enough to make many of us today reassess the gospel itself But not Paul. He believed that the righteousness of God is revealed from faith to faith. He believed these Christians had truly believed. He said of them that they were "sanctified in Christ Jesus, called to be saints" (1 Corinthians 1:2) and could be thankful "for the grace of God which is given you by Jesus Christ" (1 Corinthians 1:4). What Paul also says to them is that they were *carnal*. "And I, brethren, could not speak unto you as unto spiritual, but as unto carnal, even as unto babes in Christ.... For ye are yet carnal" (1 Corinthians 3:1, 3).

It was not salvation, then, but their inheritance in the kingdom of God that these Christians were in danger of forfeiting. So with the Galatians. Their problem was slightly different from that of the Christians at Corinth.

The Corinthians were in danger of immorality (a good synonym for "antinomianism" - lawlessness) whereas the Galatians were in danger of legalism. But the warning was the same. "They which do such things shall not inherit the kingdom of God" (Galatians 5:21). What things? "Adultery, fornication, uncleanness, lasciviousness, idolatry, witchcraft, hatred, variance, emulations. wrath, strife, seditions, heresies, envyings, murders, drunkenness, revellings, and such like" (Galatians 5:19-21). Are we to say that anybody who does any of these things (e.g. envyings, strife) is not going to heaven? Not at all. But such things as "covetousness," and "foolish talking," as well as sexual immorality, forfeit one's inheritance in God's kingdom, such having no "inheritance in the kingdom of Christ and of God" (Ephesians 5:3-5).

What is the kingdom of God? It is God's *heaven* below. Heaven is God's dwelling place. "But will God indeed dwell on the earth? behold, the heaven and heaven of heavens cannot contain thee; how much less this house that I have builded?" asked Solomon concerning the temple (1 Kings 8:27). And yet God deigned to dwell in men's hearts. "Know ye not that ye are the temple of God, and that the Spirit of God dwelleth in you?" (1 Corinthians 3:16). Heaven below is the kingdom of God. It is God dwelling in the hearts of men. For this reason the kingdom of God may be described generally as the *life of God* (regeneration) and the *conscious presence of God* (high degree of assurance). There are of course other uses of the kingdom of God in the New Testament, not the least of which is His sovereign right over any people or nation. For the kingdom of

God can be God's objective purpose whether or not the hearers accept His will.

"The kingdom of God is come nigh unto you . . . the kingdom of God is come nigh unto you" (Luke 10:9-11). "But if I with the finger of God cast out devils, no doubt the kingdom of God is come upon you" (Luke 11:20). Jesus wept over Jerusalem because Israel knew not the time of its "visitation" (Luke 19:41, 44).

I tender this thesis to the reader: The warnings of Paul relative to the kingdom of God do not remotely relate to being saved but to something else, namely, the *conscious presence of God*. The kingdom of God is heaven below. It is His life, a life which is manifested in men's hearts. Unless a person is born again, engendered with the life of God, he cannot enter into heaven below. But God's dwelling place is to be known and experienced in an immediate way. It is this wonderful way, namely, God's conscious presence, that we are called to inherit. God is a jealous God, however. "Know ye not that the friendship of the world is enmity with God?" James 4:4).

> For what fellowship hath righteousness with unrighteousness? . . . for ye are the temple of the living God; as God hath said, I will dwell in them, and walk in them; and I will be their God, and they shall be my people. Wherefore come out from among them, and be ye separate, saith the Lord, and touch not the unclean thing; and I will receive you, and will be a Father unto you, and ye shall be my sons and daughters, saith the Lord Almighty. Having therefore these promises, dearly beloved, let us cleanse ourselves from all filthiness of the flesh and spirit, perfecting holiness in the fear of God. (2 Corinthians 6:14, 16; 7:1)

There is not a single promise offered to the believer that the conscious presence of God may be inherited by a careless, frivolous, and worldly life. Not one.

Paul's use of the kingdom of God, then, is precisely the usage given in Acts 14:22. It all fits perfectly. There is no unguarded comment in Paul's epistles (nor anywhere else in God's word). It is simply that the kingdom of God, heaven below, is described in the New Testament in no fewer than four ways: first, regeneration ("born again"); second, immediate sense of His presence ("inheriting the kingdom of God"); third, His sovereign prerogative over men ("the kingdom of God is come upon you"); and fourth, when Jesus comes again (2 Timothy 4:1). It is always God's dwelling place. But when God's dwelling place is to be experienced in a powerful and wonderful way, the writers use a vast number of descriptions.

What Paul calls inheriting the kingdom of God he also calls "life everlasting" (Galatians 6:8). Is Paul contradicting John 3:16? Of course not. But as Jesus described eternal life as *knowing* the true God and His Son (John 17:3), so Paul could warn Timothy to "lay hold on eternal life" (1 Timothy 6:12). He also warns the Galatians, "Be not deceived; God is not mocked: for whatsoever a man soweth, that shall he also reap. For he that soweth to his flesh shall of the flesh reap corruption; but he that soweth to the Spirit shall of the Spirit reap life everlasting" (Galatians 6:7-8). One is not justified or saved by "not being weary in well doing." But the reaping, "if we faint not" (Galatians 6:9), is surely what Jesus called being given the "kingdom" by the Father's "good pleasure" (Luke 12:32).

131

What Paul calls inheriting the kingdom of God he also calls being "filled with the Holy Spirit" (Ephesians 5:18), the "walk in the Spirit" (Galatians 5:25), "joy in the Holy Ghost" (Romans 14:17), and the "more excellent way" (1 Corinthians 12:31—13:13). John calls it "fellowship with the Father" (1 John 1:3, 7), "abiding in the light" (1 John 2:10), "abiding in Christ" (1 John 3:6), and "perfect love" (l John 4:18). It is called "praying in the Holy Ghost" (Jude 20), "unfeigned love of the brethren" (l Peter 1:22), and "casting all your care upon him" (l Peter 5:7). James called it "counting it all joy in trials" (James 1:2) and the wisdom that "is from above" (James 3:17). It is called the "rest that remains for the people of God" (Hebrews 4:9), the peace that "passeth all understanding" (Philippians 4:7), and the "pearl of great price" (Matthew 13:46).

There is of course an inheritance that all Christians receive, namely, redemption in Christ (Ephesians 1:11). But these same Christians are enjoined to know "what is the hope of his calling, and what is the riches of the glory of his inheritance in the saints" (Ephesians 1:18). It is the latter kind of inheritance that Paul has in mind in Ephesians 5:5. To summarise: God has called us unto holiness (1 Thessalonians 4:7), which is what Paul means by walking "worthy of God, who hath called you unto his kingdom and glory" (l Thessalonians 2:12).

The greatest mistake Christians are inclined to make is to minimise the injunctions and warnings about not inheriting the kingdom of God. In other words, if you, the reader, are now saying to yourself, "I'm just glad to know I'm eternally saved—I can't be too bothered by a reward or inheriting the kingdom of God," you could not be more mistaken. "Be not deceived; God is not mocked: for whatsoever a man soweth, that shall he also reap" (Galatians 6:7). Read to the end of this book. Not inheriting the kingdom of God, heaven below, has serious ramifications at the judgment seat of Christ.

And yet it is absolutely true: once saved, always saved. God does not want us to doubt our salvation. Salvation is God's unchangeable and irrevocable gift. If anybody had reason to reassess so great salvation it was Paul when he learned what had been going on in Corinth. But his method was to reassure them more than ever that they were saved, yet to warn them in the strongest terms what it means to violate the temple of the Holy Spirit. Why are there so many warnings in the Bible about disobedience? Let 1 Corinthians 3:17 answer: "If any man defile the temple of God, him shall God destroy; for the temple of God is holy, which temple ye are." As we shall see in more detail later, such a destruction was not an eternal destruction, it was a physical destruction. Paul calls it "the destruction of the flesh" (1 Corinthians 5:5). The reason for the grave warning concerning the Lord's Supper was that these same Corinthians, some of them, had abused it again and again. "For this cause many are weak and sickly among you, and many sleep" (i.e., are dead - 1 Corinthians 11:30).

I am amazed at Paul's pastoral method. It is so different from that of so many of us today. If we find a person living in deep sin we often tend to think that threatening such a person with eternal condemnation ("You surely could not be a Christian") will work. Few stop to examine how little this method works. In my

133

Arminian days I knew certain people who backslid many times. These same people were told that if they died in a backslidden condition, they would perish in hell. It didn't make the slightest difference to them. Not the slightest. They were "filled with their own ways" (Proverbs 14:14) and were going to have their flesh satisfied if it meant going on to hell. The threat of eternal hell has little effect upon the backslider.

But what made Peter sob his heart out right after he had denied that he even knew Jesus was that Jesus "looked" at him (Luke 22:61-62). Peter knew that the Lord still loved him.

However, God wanted Peter to learn obedience. God is serious about sanctification. It is true that sanctification was not a prerequisite for glorification, or Paul would have placed it in line with "calling" and "justification" (Romans 8:30). And yet he said, "This is the will of God, even your sanctification" (1 Thessalonians 4:3) and warned against despising such holiness (1 Thessalonians 4:8). "Without which [holiness] no man shall see the Lord" (Hebrews 12:14). God therefore has taken measures that guarantee that His people are holy. They are called chastening.

8

God's Chastening

In the summer of 1956, I underwent the first major trial of my life as a Christian. (I had had trials before then, of course, but not as a direct consequence of following Jesus.) The experience of October 31, 1955 not only gave me a heightened assurance of salvation but led me into a new theological world which, as I have said, I thought had not been discovered by anyone since the apostle Paul! What I perceived to be true in the Bible was not upheld by anybody I knew at the time. I resigned my first pastorate, which was in Palmer, Tennessee, in May 1956 and came home from my college in Nashville later that month, planning never to return. With my newly-discovered truths I felt my old college had no further contribution to make at that time. In the meantime my friends distanced themselves from me and my relatives were grieved. My grandmother had given me a new car upon my becoming the pastor of a church, but she asked me to return the car now that I was taking a different direction. My own father was heart-broken. One relative actually called me a "disgrace to the family." I had not known such treatment or loneliness.

I was not prepared for it. God had not told me this would happen.

One July afternoon in Ashland, Kentucky, I fell across my bed in despair. It seemed I had no friends. I had no future. All I had tried to do in the preceding months was to follow the Lord. "Why, Lord?" I cried as I lay on that bed. What followed was something that has happened only once or twice since. I emphasise that because I would not want to mislead the reader into thinking this is a common experience with me (for it certainly is not). But in that hour of deep need I suddenly felt impelled to turn to Hebrews 12:6, having no idea at all what it said. I quickly turned to my Bible and read: "For whom the Lord loveth he chasteneth, and scourgeth every son whom he receiveth." That was my introduction to the doctrine of God's chastening, which I had not heard of before.

I suspect that one of the most underestimated teachings in the Bible is the doctrine of chastening. I hope the reader will never feel quite the same about it after reading this book. Hebrews 12:6 summarises this teaching. The word chasten means "to correct by punishment." The word scourge means "to whip with thongs." The writer's plain statement is this: whom the Lord loves He chastens; therefore, every child of God will, sooner or later, experience God's chastening.

God's chastening is not punishment for its own sake, but always to correct. It always has a definite aim: to correct, to equip, to prepare for something around the corner. God's chastening is preparation. In a word, chastening always has a *redemptive* purpose. It is never carried out by God to "get even" with us. God "got even" at the cross. This is why the psalmist could say, "As far as the east is from the west, so far hath he removed our transgressions from us" (Psalm 103:12). Chastening ought not to be regarded as God's way of satisfying Himself. Parents do this, yes. "We have had fathers of our flesh which corrected us, and we gave them reverence . . . for they verily for a few days chastened us after their own pleasure" (Hebrews 12:9-10). We parents chasten our own with partly selfish motives. We may even lose our tempers with our children, and at our best we are partly thinking of the reward we will get later (if only by having others compliment us). But not so with God. He chastens us entirely "for our profit, that we might be partakers of his holiness" (Hebrews 12:10).

Holiness. That is the purpose of God in chastening us. For the writer continues: "follow peace with all men, and holiness, without which no man shall see the Lord" (Hebrews 12:14). None of us takes to holiness "naturally." We are all congenitally allergic to holiness. It is easier to watch television than it is to pray, easier to read a magazine than to read the Bible. All of us have a tendency to impute more spirituality to ourselves than is there. Chastening is so often the only way by which we see ourselves with true objectivity.

God is the only infallible parent. He never loses His temper. "For the wrath of man worketh not the righteousness of God" (James 1:20). God always keeps His "cool."

When He metes out chastening, it is carefully designed, carefully planned, carefully thought out. For God chastens for one reason only: for our good. It is not for Himself but "for our profit" (Hebrews 12:10).

Why is it that we tend to underestimate God's chastening? I think it is this: Our tendency is to think in terms of heaven or hell, and if we know we are going to heaven, we worry about little else. We, therefore, find it rather easy to dismiss His chastening. This is because we underestimate how awful it can be. As we shall see, there are various levels of chastening, but I can safely state that, whatever level may be our lot, "no chastening for the present seemeth to be joyous, but grievous" (Hebrews 12:11). Chastening can be very painful indeed. Only a fool would underestimate it, but all of us have been fools at one time or another. Chastening is painful—grievous rugged. Sometimes it would even seem ruthless.

"Verily thou art a God that hidest thyself, O God of Israel, the Saviour (Isaiah 45:15). That which largely makes chastening chastening is the sudden hiding of God's face. As John Newton put it:

How tedious and tasteless the hours
When Jesus no longer I see;
Sweet prospects, sweet birds and sweet flowers
Have all lost their sweetness to me.

God does not give advance warning that He will hide His face; He just does it. He never says, "Look here, My child, next Thursday afternoon about 3 o'clock you will begin to notice that I am withdrawing the light of my countenance." Never. No warning. He just does it. Often for no apparent reason! But there is a reason. "Afterward it yieldeth the peaceable fruit of righteousness unto them which are exercised thereby" (Hebrews 12:11).

138

And yet it does not follow that, merely because chastening does not "satisfy" God (only the blood of Jesus does that), there is still no further cause for our being chastened. Indeed, the doctrine of chastening, not unlike what we have seen with other New Testament teachings, can be usefully understood in terms of "causes." There are three causes that will bear our looking into: first, the teleological cause (the end that God has in mind), which is that we should be partakers of God's holiness; second, the underlying cause, our unpreparedness; and, in many instances, third, the precipitating cause, a specific sin on our part which brings on God's chastening.

First, the underlying cause gives God the liberty to chasten us at any moment. It is our sinfulness moreover that justifies God in hiding His face from us without advance notice. "If we say that we have no sin, we deceive ourselves, and the truth is not in us" (1 John 1:8). Walking in the light does not remove sin, it cleanses it; and if we say that we are not sinful, we are deceived. Chastening often is but designed to show us how sinful we are. Second, such sinfulness lies behind our unpreparedness and this should serve notice to all of us that God is just and faithful when He suddenly chastens us. In other words, He needs no "reason" as such. He always has reason: we are sinners.

However, there is often a third cause for God's chastising us: a specific sin which we have committed which sometimes "forces" God to deal with us. Not that God chastens us for every sin. He does not. "He hath not dealt with us after our sins; nor rewarded us according to our iniquities" (Psalm 103:10). If He dealt with us according to our sins, we would have been dead long before now. It is a fact: God does not chastise us for each and every sin we have committed. It is with stunned amazement that I contemplate this. I often think of Ezra's prayer: "O my God, I am ashamed and blush to lift up my face to thee, my God: for our iniquities are increased over our head, and our trespass is grown up unto the heavens . . . seeing that thou our God hast punished us less than our iniquities deserve, and hast given us such deliverance as this" (Ezra 9:6, 13).

We may safely conclude that God is not interested in "getting even." Nothing could be more ridiculous. But why does He chasten us for some sins and not for others? I do not know for sure. But I know that it is true. Perhaps we could give these answers.

First, God does not chasten us for every sin as a bold demonstration that He has no desire to get even. He was absolutely satisfied by the blood of His Son at the cross. The "eye for an eye and tooth for a tooth" has no attraction for Him.

Second, He chastens us for some of our sins as a sign that He is dealing with us and has not abandoned us. It was a most high compliment to Jonah that he was "found out" by the mariners on the ship (Jonah 1:7). If God let us get away with every disobedience, we should have good reason to ask, "Does He love us at all?" I heard recently of a child who said to his teacher at school, "I don't think my parents love me for they never punish me."

Third, God apparently chastens us for those sins that damage His church and bring His own name into reproach. I suspect that it is at this point we come close to understanding God's ways. God is jealous for His name. He is also jealous for the reputation of His own enterprise in the world. The incestuous man in Corinth persisted in a sin which "is not so much as named among the Gentiles" (1 Corinthians 5:1). One reason behind David's chastening (owing to his adultery and sin of murder) was this: "because by this deed thou hast given great occasion to the enemies of the Lord to blaspheme, the child also that is born unto thee shall surely die" (2 Samuel 12:14). The one thing above all else which God will not have is to put the name of His Son "to an open shame" (Hebrews 6:6).

Fourth, God delights in vindicating His servants who have been hurt. If we have hurt others, we are exceedingly apt to be found out and to be dealt with openly. God is grieved when any of His own children have been abused. He is no respecter of persons (Colossians 3:25) and there is not a single one of us among His family who is God's "favourite". Such partiality does not exist in the family of God. If you have been hurt by another, God will vindicate you if you leave it to Him alone, "seeing it is a righteous thing with God to recompense tribulation to them that trouble you" (2 Thessalonians 1:6). All of us would do well to examine ourselves in the light of the possibility we have hurt another of God's children.

Finally, God seems to "discover" (or expose - see Lamentations 4:22) those sins that compete most with His own will in our lives. "Let us lay aside every weight, and the sin which doth so easily beset us" (Hebrews 12:1). God knows us infinitely better than we know ourselves. He has a fresh "computer printout" on our personality and feelings every second of the day. He knows when we need the slap on the wrist or the rugged grabbing of the shoulders - or the seemingly ruthless slamming into an icy-cold dungeon. He is quite able to do such. But it is always for our good - "for our profit, that we might be partakers of his holiness" (Hebrews 12:10).

There are some who want to say that God takes no notice of our sins because they are buried in the sea of God's forgetfulness. If God has washed away our sins by the blood of Christ, how can He possibly notice them? After all, did not David speak of the man "to whom the Lord will not impute sin" (Psalm 32:1-2; cf. Romans 4:7-8)? If God imputes "no sin" to us, how can He possibly chasten us for sin? I answer that He chastened David Himself. Furthermore, why would our Lord give us the prayer, "Forgive us our trespasses" (Matthew 6:12) if we would be confessing what God did not see? Why also did Jesus say, "If ye forgive not men their trespasses, neither will your Father forgive your trespasses" (Matthew 6:15)?

There are two kinds of forgiveness of sins in the New Testament. One pertains to our eternal salvation (justification by faith), the other to our temporal fellowship with the Father. Insofar as our eternal salvation is concerned, yes, our sins are washed away and will not be held against us. It does not follow however that God does not see what sins we commit after our conversion. He does see them. Paul never intended that the glorious doctrine of justification should remove the possibility of committing actual sin in this life. "Shall we continue in sin, that grace may abound? God forbid" (Romans 6:1-

2). "Let not sin therefore reign in your mortal body that ye should obey it in the lusts thereof" (Romans 6:12). Paul warned the Thessalonians against continuing in sexual sin, "because that the Lord is the avenger of all such, as we also have forewarned you and testified" (1 Thessalonians 4:6). There is nothing more absurd than to say that, because we are justified before God and hence are "new men in Christ," we are regarded in our daily walk with the Lord as being without sin. "If we say that we have no sin, we deceive ourselves, and the truth is not in us" (1 John 1:8).

The teleological cause for God's chastening is that we should be partakers of His holiness. The underlying cause is our general sinfulness or unpreparedness. But there is often an immediate or precipitating cause the very sins we commit. If there were no sin in us, there would never be any chastening. If we never committed sins, God would never be angry with us. But he could be angry with David: "O Lord, rebuke me not in thine anger, neither chasten me in thy hot displeasure" (Psalm 6:1).

We must never underestimate God's chastening, neither should we underestimate how important it is to God that we should be holy. "Because it is written, Be ye holy; for I am holy" (1 Peter 1:16). Indeed, "Follow peace with all men, and holiness, without which no man shall see the Lord" (Hebrews 12:14). It is in this very matter that chastening comes into the picture. God is so serious about our inheriting the kingdom of God that He has taken definite measures to ensure that we enter it - one way or another. Those who have been justified shall be "glorified" (Romans 8:30).

But holiness or sanctification is not effectual in God's "golden chain" of redemption. Calling is. Justification is. Glorification is. These are effectual - that is, inevitable by sovereign grace alone. That is what Romans 8:30 is all about. But the sanctification which God has for us is by our "co-operation." Sanctification does not come by irresistible grace. It is what we do in voluntary response to God's grace. But if we do not willingly respond to His beckoning call to be like Jesus, He has a way of hemming us in, boxing us in, so that we become very willing indeed.

The lack of progress in holiness, then, calls for God's chastening rod. But as sanctification is not irresistible, neither is God's chastening necessarily effectual at first. When we do not heed God's warnings, He must take stricter measures with us. Some sins are worse than others. There is a sin "not unto death" but also a "sin unto death" (1 John 5:16-17). As some sins are worse than others, so some measures of chastisement are more rugged than others. "For this cause many are weak and sickly among you, and many sleep," said Paul to those who were abusing the Lord's Supper (1 Corinthians 11:30). From this we may gather how serious God is about the obedience of His children.

Whatever else we are to learn regarding God's chastening, this must be said: "the judgments of the Lord are true and righteous altogether" (Psalm 19:9). For chastening is God's righteous judgment. He never makes a mistake, He never misfires. To the one who is warned by His righteous judgment comes the sweet realisation that such is "more to be desired . . . than gold, yea, than much fine gold; sweeter also than honey and the honeycomb"

(Psalm 19:10). That is why the writer could say, "Despise not thou the chastening of the Lord, nor faint when thou art rebuked of him" (Hebrews 12:5). Such chastening is an encouragement. It shows that we are being dealt with by a loving Father.

But God's judgments are also a warning. "By them is thy servant warned: and in keeping of them there is great reward" (Psalm 19:11). God's chastening can therefore be preventative medicine. His judgments are designed to spare us even more grief. If we take the hint from His judgments, "in keeping of them there is great reward." But if we show contempt for His warning, it only means harsher measures in this life, and in the end, alas, the fiery judgment of His indignation at the judgment seat of Christ (1 Corinthians 3:13; Hebrews 10:27).

There is this principle which I believe will safely carry us through in our understanding of God's chastening, summed up in Paul's words: "if we would judge ourselves, we should not be judged" (1 Corinthians 11:31). This means that if we deal with our sin before God has to, we shall be completely spared His fierce judgment later on. God does not chasten us for a sin we have truly repented of. The way to deal with our sin is by "walking in the light" (1 John 1:7).

In other words, the best way to avoid the hot wrath of God's chastening is via the surgery of His word. "For the word of God is quick, and powerful, and sharper than any two-edged sword" (Hebrews 4:12). The best way to have God deal with our sin is in many cases through the "public" surgery of His word - preaching. It is the mildest form of chastening that there is - just letting His word do its work!

There are basically three kinds of chastening: internal, external, and terminal. The internal chastening is when God's pure word cuts through to our hearts and we submit to His surgery. The internal chastening of the Lord is always secret. Nobody knows about it but us. It may be open-heart surgery but it is still secret. When God's chastening comes via His word - whether through preaching, teaching, good books, or just reading the Bible - it is a wonderful thing. It is also between us and God alone. The best way to have God deal with our sin is for us to take His word seriously and thus spare ourselves much sorrow. "Thy word is a lamp unto my feet, and a light unto my path. I have sworn, and I will perform it, that I will keep thy righteous judgments" (Psalm 119:105-106). "Before I was afflicted I went astray: but now have I kept thy word" (Psalm 119:67).

External chastening is not so secret. It is partly what David meant by God's "hot displeasure" (Psalm 38:1). David feared this, but it is the only recourse God has when we don't take heed to His word. Jonah could have spared himself so much trouble had he gone to Nineveh the first time. God said "go" and Jonah said "no" Jonah 1:2-3). God's external chastening is not secret, but His open arena where others are often given to see our folly. Jonah was found out by the mariners on the ship he had boarded for Tarshish (Jonah 1:7). David was found out by Nathan the prophet (2 Samuel 12:7). Zachariah was found out by Gabriel the archangel (Luke 1:20). Moses was found out by his brethren (Exodus 2:14). Peter was found out by the crowing of a cockerel in the distance (Matthew 26:75). The incestuous man of Corinth was found out by the apostle Paul (1 Corinthians 5:1-5).

146

Ananias and Sapphira were found out by Peter (Acts 5:1-11). Peter was later found out by Paul - "I said unto Peter before them all" (Galatians 2:14).

There is also an external chastening which may not be so apparent to others but which is not merely the operation of God's word on our hearts. It may be connected to God's outward providence - like sickness, trouble, financial loss, calamity - but which is known only to the person himself. I call this external, as opposed to internal, because it is a chastening that is open, outward, physical, and material. Yet it need not be known to all that it is a case of God's chastening. God may spare one public disclosure at first. But we must be cautious here. Not all trouble or calamity is due to a specific sin. Job is a proof of that (Job 1:1). It would be a very hasty assumption indeed if one regarded all adversity as a result of God's displeasure with us. But it is nonetheless true that in some instances God can chasten openly (as opposed to inwardly) without others necessarily knowing what you know, namely, that God has kindly chosen to deal with you. "Wherefore doth a living man complain, a man for the punishment of his sins? (Lamentations 3:39). It is far better to have God expose your sin while you are alive than at the judgment seat of Christ.

This leads us to terminal chastening. I call it terminal chastening for two reasons. First, because it is something which takes place beyond the present age. It takes place on the last day. Secondly, it can justly be called a terminal chastening because one's loss of reward at the judgment seat of Christ will never be regained throughout the endless aeons of eternity. In other words, one will spend eternity "rewardless" in heaven. It will be an everlasting reminder that one was saved "so as by fire" (1 Corinthians 3:15). We shall deal with this in the next chapter. Let it suffice to say here that the judgment seat of Christ for some will but mean the ultimate measure of God's chastening. It will be such for those who simply would not heed the previous warnings of God in their lifetime. We can further see why we have the eloquent question of Lamentations 3:39: "Wherefore doth a *living* man complain, a man for the punishment of his sins?"

I should fervently hope that one great benefit of this book (perhaps an unexpected blessing) will be to warn the reader of the seriousness of disobedience. If you thought that the thesis of this book once saved, always saved would allow you to feel good about yourself while you wade knee-deep in sin, you could not be more wrong. "For we shall all stand before the judgment seat of Christ" (Romans 14:10). It is much, much better to deal with your sin now than then. For "if we would judge ourselves, we should not be judged" (1 Corinthians 11:31). Perhaps this word has reached you in the very nick of time?

There is an intimate connection between chastening and backsliding. Backsliding can be defined as *slipping back from the revealed will of God*. The will of God is revealed in His word. No man is above the word. God is no respecter of persons. Nobody is exempt from the plain teachings of scripture as our guide to how to live our lives. No one. Chastening is designed to prevent backsliding. But it can also be the result of backsliding. As we have said, our own sin can be the immediate or

148

precipitating cause of chastening. There is in fact such a thing as a needless chastening. We could easily avoid a certain amount of chastisement.

And yet all of us have backslid to some degree at some time or another. We've all done things we wish we hadn't done. All of us have skeletons in our closets. Backsliding is done by degrees. On a scale, let us say, from one to ten (the latter being the most extreme case), who among us can claim exemption from any stage? Do you never experience any of the following: succumbing to flattery, nurturing a hurt feeling, holding a grudge, losing your temper, having sudden motivation by love of money, being a respecter of persons, not witnessing when you should have, doubting God, committing adultery in your heart (lusting), showing contempt for the poor, name-dropping, feeling jealous (or making another feel jealous), having selfish ambition under the pretext of doing God's will, having self-vindication, feeling racially superior, being bitter, coveting, super-imposing God's name on your own selfish enterprise, withholding a portion of your tithe, talking yourself too seriously, not walking in the light, judging another, not being able to forgive and forget, being governed by a spirit of fear, being a cause of stumbling, overeating, acting arrogantly, gossiping, not speaking to someone you don't particularly like, feeling good over another's disappointment or lack of success, not rejoicing when Christ is preached (if you don't agree with the preacher or his church), esteeming yesterday's prophet while rejecting today's prophet, being pious to be seen of men, not waiting for answered prayer, keeping a mental record of wrongs, being a snob, feeling superior to

149

another person's class or education, looking for a chance to get even, hurting another's reputation or influence, withholding a good word about another, pouting in self-pity, having an inability to rejoice with those that rejoice, defending class distinction, being selective regarding those you witness to or invite to church, justifying yourself when your own sin is exposed, not building up your own minister, not praying sincerely that God *will bless* your enemy, murmuring or complaining about a trial, engendering strife.

Perhaps my list is ridiculously long. But let it demonstrate how common backsliding is. I would be afraid to say which of the above sins is a one or a ten. Any one of them, if not brought into check, would almost certainly become a ten. In other words, if repentance does not follow sooner or later, any sin will lead to absolute disaster.

Spirituality brings sin into check, closing the gap between sin and repentance. Repentance is agreeing with God. It comes from a Greek word *(metanoia)* which means "change of mind." Repentance is saying, "I was wrong, I will now do God's will." Spirituality seeks to close the gap in time between sin and repentance. I will illustrate what I mean: the less spiritual I am, the longer it will take to confess "I was wrong." The more spiritual I am, the less time it will take to admit "I was wrong." Some of us take years before we finally come round to admitting how wrong we were. Some take months. Some take weeks. Some take days. Some take hours. Some take minutes. Some take seconds. When we reach the stage of perceiving our sin in seconds, we are less prone to sin at all. We can catch ourselves just before it happens.

John calls this "abiding in Christ." "Whosoever abideth in him sinneth not: whosoever sinneth hath not seen him, neither known him" (1 John 3:6). However surprising this may come to the reader, John claims that it is possible not to sin. He does not mean that we never sin (1 John 1:10 and 2:1-2 prove this) but he does mean that at the moment when we are abiding in Christ we are not sinning-at least not then. This is not a reference to positional righteousness John is not referring to our eternal justification before God), it refers to our state—our actual spiritual condition—at the moment. When he says "whosoever sinneth hath not seen him, neither known him" he means that such sinful conduct or attitude betrays the actual condition of your heart at that moment. Do not claim God as being behind your actions when you act like that, says John.

Obviously John does not mean such a person was never saved or he would be repudiating his own words in 1 John 2:1-2. John's statement is designed to force us to disdain God or our own lofty spirituality as the source of any wrongdoing. In other words, all of us have a tendency to claim God is with us and on our side no matter what we do. You cannot do that, says John. You show you are not walking with the Lord at all.

In my pastoral experience I have had people sincerely claim God's approval for what the Bible dearly calls sin. "We've prayed a lot about it," they will tell me without batting an eyelid. John will not let people get away with that. Spirituality leads people to call sin sin and it seeks to dose the gap in time between the occasion of sin and true repentance.

As to back-sliding being by degrees on a scale from one to ten—I would suggest that the seriousness of backsliding is largely determined by its outward effect on others. Many of the sins on my aforementioned list can be committed secretly in the heart. But it is when they are carried out openly before others that they are obviously more serious.

Some want to dismiss the issue by saying "sin is sin" and "all sin is equally abhorrent in God's sight." That is not true. Some sins are worse than others. This is borne out by the Levitical law and New Testament practice. That John said that there is a sin *not* unto death (1 John 5:17) shows that there is such a thing as a lesser sin. Jesus spoke of "the greater sin" (John 19:11). As we have already seen, Paul was shocked that in the church he founded at Corinth there was sin "as is not so much as named among the Gentiles, that one should have his father's wife" (1 Corinthians 5:1). Some sins are worse than others. Why? Because some are more damaging than others. Some sins hurt people more than other sins, and, most of all, some sins are more damaging to the reputation and influence of God's church. When the honour of God's name is brought into question, we can expect God to step in at some stage. How He may do this may vary from person to person, from place to place, from church to church, and from generation to generation.

I have no idea what God's scale is. I do believe however that He has one. It is known only to Him. How He responds in heaven to our sins from "one" to "five" and what He would regard as "ten," I do not know. Such may well vary from person to person. What one can get

152

away with and others are severely chastened for is entirely God's business. I am sure that many have said no when God said go and were not swallowed-up by a great fish. It does not follow however that such are not dealt with. The one thing in any case worse than not being swallowed-up by a great fish is not apparently being dealt with at all. The one thing worse than God's hot wrath is His cold justice. "Who can stand before his cold?" (Psalm 147:17). God's "cold shoulder" is a thousand times worse than His obvious hot displeasure. I would much prefer to know that He is angry with me than for Him to be angry with me and not let me know it.

For if God seems to cease to deal with us, it does not mean that He hasn't taken judgment. On the contrary, it may mean that the worst thing of all has happened—that He has sworn in His wrath. When God does that, it is something done behind the scenes. It is secret. When God swore in His wrath towards His own people whom He saved out of Egypt, it was not understood for several generations. It was later revealed to the psalmist but not to the children of Israel at the time (Psalm 95:7-11). All that was known at the time was that the same people who faithfully kept the Passover were now dying in the wilderness (1 Corinthinans 10:5; Hebrews 3:17). They simply did not gain the inheritance that ought to have been theirs: they did not enter God's "rest" (Hebrews 3:11).

It would be a serious mistake to dismiss the children of Israel in the wilderness by writing them off as unregenerate from the start. To say that such people were never saved is to fly in the face of the memorable fact that they kept the Passover. They obeyed Moses, who gave an unprecedented, if not strange, command to sprinkle lamb's blood on either side and over their doors (Exodus 12:7). But they did it and God delivered them from Pharaoh by a high hand (Exodus 14:8). If obeying Moses' command to sprinkle blood on the night of the Passover was not a type of saving faith, I do not know what is. These people were saved. We shall see them in heaven even if it turns out they were "saved so as by fire" (1 Corinthians 3:15).

It certainly fitted the apostle's position and the manner in which he was having to deal with these carnal souls at Corinth. It is not surprising that he should use them for an illustration of castaways (1 Corinthians 9:27), having had to deal with the case of that incestuous man (1 Corinthians 5:5). Thus he reminded his hearers that all the children of Israel left Egypt *"all* our fathers were under the cloud, and *all* passed through the sea; and were *all* baptised unto Moses in the cloud and in the sea; and did *all* eat the same spiritual meat; and did *all* drink the same spiritual drink: for they drank of that spiritual Rock that followed them: and *that Rock was Christ"* (1 Corinthians 10:1-4).

But with many of them "God was not well pleased" (1 Corinthians 10:5). Certain ones spied out the promised land of Canaan. Caleb said, "Let us go up at once, and possess it; for we are well able to overcome it" (Numbers 13:30). But Caleb was outnumbered. The majority won—the people of Canaan were regarded by the majority as giants, "and we were in our own sight as grasshoppers, and so we were in their sight" (Numbers 13:33). The children of Israel forfeited the very inheri-

154

tance that God had promised them. Jude pointed out, "how that the Lord, having saved the people out of the land of Egypt, afterward destroyed them that believed not" (literally, "believed not the second time" - Gr. *deutron* - Jude 5). Behind the scenes God said, "I sware in my wrath, They shall not enter into my rest" (Hebrews 3:11).

From the account of the children of Israel in the wilderness there emerges a picture, or pattern, by which God's dealings with every Christian can be gauged. At what stage during the forty-year period God swore in His wrath we do not know. What we know is that at some point along the way, presumably after Caleb was outnumbered, God removed Canaan utterly from the picture for those children of Israel. Caleb and Joshua were exceptions. God's rest is a type of our inheritance in the kingdom of God. Losing our inheritance below is tantamount to losing our reward above and will result in the severest type of chastening, namely, being saved "so as by fire" (1 Corinthians 3:15).

Not gaining our inheritance in the kingdom of God may be a completely painless matter at the time. This is what is so scary. God might not do anything drastic as He did with Ananias and Sapphira (Acts 5:1-11). We simply may not know what we have missed until we face God at the judgment seat of Christ. On the other hand, to appear to come short of our inheritance may in some cases be most painful indeed. The man in Corinth that we have mentioned was to receive the news that he had been delivered unto Satan by none other than the apostle Paul (1 Corinthians 5:5). He was completely shattered by this news. That this man was saved is obvious not

155

only by his repentance later (2 Corinthians 2:7) but by Paul's words even before he knew that the man might repent: "Deliver such an one unto Satan for the destruction of the flesh, that the spirit may be saved in the day of the Lord Jesus" (1 Corinthinans 5:5). Some have regarded 1 Corinthians 5:5 as the strongest verse in the Bible for once saved, always saved and I would not disagree.

We will not know until we get to heaven who wrote the epistle to the Hebrews, but, whoever it was, he was governed by the exact same theology as that behind Paul's delivering the man in Corinth to Satan. Paul was convinced at the time that this incestuous man had "fallen away" so as to be beyond hope of repentance (cf. Hebrews 6:6). Paul had to do what he did but seemed quite surprised later to learn that the same man had repented - which only showed that the man was not yet in the awful category of Hebrews 6:4-6 after all. Thus the man in Corinth appeared to have fallen away but only God knows who really has. This should make every one of us cautious. Only God knows who cannot be renewed again to repentance.

God could have sworn in His wrath regarding David the moment he lay in Bathsheba's bed (2 Samuel 11:4), or the moment he gave orders to have Uriah murdered (2 Samuel 11:15). Had God sworn in His wrath concerning David, it might have resulted in David's "getting away with it." If so, would David have been better off ? No. Neither would the name of God (2 Samuel 12:14). This seems to be why God visited Ananias and Sapphira with sudden death (Acts 5:1-11). I am aware that some do not believe Ananias and Sapphira were ever truly converted. But, there is not a single passage in Acts that leads us to believe that Ananias and Sapphira were not genuine believers in the Lord Jesus Christ.

The same is true of Simon Magus. We know he believed (Acts 8:13). Luke in writing the account of Acts does not lead us to think that Simon was insincere when he believed. Simon Magus's response to Peter's statement ("I perceive that thou art in the gall of bitterness, and in the bond of iniquity") could be interpreted as that of a serious believer, "Pray ye to the Lord for me, that none of these things which ye have spoken come upon me" (Acts 8:23-24). On the other hand, it may be that Ananias and Sapphira were never saved and that Simon Magus was a hypocrite from the start. We will know about them when we get to heaven.

All I would point out is that what is equally credible about Ananias, Sapphira, and Simon Magus is what was unquestionably true of Simon Peter before them, that they were saved but gave in to the flesh - as any Christian is prone to do at some stage. In any case, there are only three possible interpretations I am aware of: first, they were never saved; second, they were saved but lost their salvation and will be in hell throughout eternity; third, they were saved but lost their reward or inheritance in the kingdom of God. For all I know Simon Magus was given time to prove himself. We do not need these particular examples to substantiate the truth expounded in this chapter. But I pose the possibility that they were examples of God's external, if not terminal, chastening.

The worst mistake we can make is to underestimate the seriousness of God's chastening. "It is a fearful thing to fall into the hands of the living God" (Hebrews 10:31). But, best of all, chastening is the exclusive heritage of God's own children - not the unsaved. "The Lord shall judge his people" (Hebrews 10:30).

His judgments are "true and righteous altogether" (Psalm 19:9). Thus when it comes to His judgment to chasten, we know that He only has one type of person in mind: "for whom the Lord loveth he chasteneth, and scourgeth every son whom he receiveth" (Hebrews 12:6).

9

The Judgement Seat Of Christ

If God's chastening is the most underestimated teaching in the New Testament, the final judgment of God is probably the most neglected. What the Old Testament prophets called the "day of the Lord" (e.g., Joel 3:14; Amos 5:18) the New Testament calls "that day" (Matthew 7:22), "the last day" (John 12:48), "the day" (Romans 2:16), "a day" (Acts 17:31), "the day of our Lord Jesus Christ" (1 Corinthians 1:8), "the day of the Lord Jesus" (1 Corinthians 5:5), "the day of Jesus Christ" (Philippians 1:6), "the day of the Lord" (1 Thessalonians 5:2), "day of Christ" (2 Thessalonians 2:2), "the day of judgment" (2 Peter 2:9; 1 John 4:17), and "the day of God" (2 Peter 3:12).

The apostle Paul borrowed a term that was common in his day and applied it to God's final judgment - the judgment seat. In the Greek it is the word *bema*. The bema seat in Corinth was a large, richly-decorated rostrum, centrally located in the marketplace. It was the place where rewards were given out - garlands, trophies, crowns, etc. - but also punishments. Thus, in writing to the Corinthians Paul said, "For we must all appear before the judgment seat [*bema*] of Christ; that every one may receive the things done in his body, according to that he hath done, whether it be good or bad" (2 Corinthians 5:10). So to the Romans Paul wrote, "We shall all stand before the judgment seat [*bema*] of Christ" (some manuscripts say "judgment seat of God" - (Romans 14:10).

The New Testament writers held in common the conviction that there would be a final judgment and that such would reveal the truth of God and of men—of God's ways and of men's hearts. Many of us tend to gloss over such statements as these. "For there is nothing covered, that shall not be revealed; neither hid, that shall not be known. Therefore whatsoever ye have spoken in darkness shall be heard in the light; and that which ye have spoken in the ear in closets shall be proclaimed upon the housetops" (Luke 12:2-3; cf. Luke 8:17; Matthew 10:26; Mark 4:22).

Paul was willing to forfeit any personal vindication for the time being: after all, "I judge not mine own self . . . He that judgeth me is the Lord. Therefore judge nothing before the time, until the Lord come, who both will bring to light the hidden things of darkness, and will make manifest the counsels of the hearts and then shall every man have praise of God" (1 Corinthians 4:3-5). Peter said that "judgment must begin at the house of God: and if it first begin at us, what shall the end be of them that obey not the gospel of God? And if the righteous scarcely be saved, where shall the ungodly and the sinner appear?" (l Peter 4:17-18).

There is yet another strain in the New Testament that seems to be almost completely neglected in Christian literature the matter of rewards. It is strange that so prominent a matter should be almost completely overlooked by many of us. Jesus could say, "Great is your reward in heaven" (Matthew 5:12). "He that receiveth a prophet in the name of a prophet shall receive a prophet's reward; and he that receiveth a righteous man in the name of a righteous man shall receive a righteous man's reward. And whosoever shall give to drink unto one of these little ones a cup of cold water only in the name of a disciple, verily I say unto you, he shall in no wise lose his reward" (Matthew 10:41-42). "For the Son of man shall come in the glory of his Father with his angels; and then he shall reward every man according to his works" (Matthew 16:27). "But love ye your enemies, and do good, and lend, hoping for nothing again; and your reward shall be great, and ye shall be the children of the Highest for he is kind unto the unthankful and to the evil (Luke 6:35).

The New Testament writers took the matter of rewards seriously. But many of us today seem to think the idea of rewards is beneath us. We seem almost embarrassed to speak of rewards. We act as though such a concept is repugnant to the sovereign grace of God or to Christian maturity. Surely only a child, some say, is motivated by the idea of a "prize" or a "reward." Let Jesus answer: "Except ye be converted, and become as little children, ye shall not enter into the kingdom of heaven" (Matthew 18:3). The great apostle Paul was very exercised over the idea of "reward" (1 Corinthians 9:17-18) or "prize" (Philippians 3:14; 1 Corinthians 9:24) or "crown" (2 Timothy 4:8; 1 Corinthians 9:25). James sought to motivate us in the light of the possibility of "the crown of life" (James 1:12) and Peter by the "crown of glory" (1 Peter 5:4).

It is argued by some that the parable of the vineyard militates against the concept of reward in heaven. After all, it is pointed out, those who came in at the eleventh hour received the same as those who had worked all day long (Matthew 20:1-16). It is usually overlooked by such interpreters that all who worked in the vineyard had "agreed" for a certain wage (Matthew 20:2, 13). Moreover, the point of the parable is to demonstrate that it is God's sovereign prerogative to do as He pleases with each of us. "Is it not lawful for me to do what I will with mine own ? (Matthew 20:15). The marvellous truth of the parable of the vineyard demonstrates that not only may anyone be saved and made fit for heaven just before he dies (see Luke 23:43 - Jesus words to the dying thief on the cross), but also that it is possible for a young Christian (in terms of time of service) to receive the same "crown" as the aged, mature Christian who has served the Lord for fifty years. For Paul simply said that the crown of righteousness was "not to me only, but unto all them also that *love his appearing*" (2 Timothy 4:8). The parable of the vineyard gives all of us hope that God can even use the backslider at the last moment. Samson's finest hour was in his death (Judges 16:30) and he even earned a place in Hebrews 11 as a man of faith (Hebrews 11:32).

God is the "righteous judge" (2 Timothy 4:8). His chastening can vary from person to person as also His secret will for each of us. When Peter was told how he would die, he could not resist enquiring how John would die. But Jesus replied, "If I will that he tarry till I come, what is that to thee ? follow thou me" (John 21:18-22).

As the will of God may vary from person to person, it should not be surprising if God gives rewards in much the same way. Arthur Blessitt may be commanded by the Lord to carry an eighty-pound twelve-foot cross all over the world - suffering awful persecution and winning untold hundreds to the Lord - while another remains at home. Whether or not Arthur's reward will be greater in heaven I do not know (I would not be surprised if it is greater), but I am sure of this: there is such a thing as rewards in heaven. *"We* must *all* appear before the judgment seat of Christ; that *everyone* may receive the things *done in his body,* according to that he hath done, whether it be *good or bad"* (2 Corinthians 5:10). This is a plain warning but also encouragement to every Christian - and Paul included himself.

I only wish that the sight of God's bema seat would have the same effect on all of us that it had upon Paul. For he immediately added, "Knowing therefore the terror of the Lord, we persuade men" (2 Corinthians 5:11). If somehow we could see the judgment seat of Christ as Paul saw it, I reckon it would do for us what it did for him. I do not see how anybody could get the slightest glimpse of this without being profoundly affected by it.

Before we proceed any further in this chapter, I want to say three things plainly and candidly. First, I do not know precisely what is meant by reward, prize or crown. Second, I do not know what is meant by the fire that is said to be manifested in that day. Third, I do not wish to delve into the details of eschatology (the doctrine of last things), precisely when and where the bema seat of

Christ takes place in God's eternal scheme. I agree with the man who said that we will know a lot more about heaven five minutes after we are there than all the speculation can tell us this side of heaven. I suspect this is equally true of the Judgment Seat of Christ. But if we can but capture the seriousness of it and not go beyond what the New Testament writers actually say, this chapter can be of some benefit to our Christian lives.

What is inescapable is this: The same man who, more than any other writer in the New Testament, carefully demonstrated that we are eternally saved by the imputed righteousness of Christ also said that at Christ's bema seat every one of us shall receive the things done in his body, according to what he has done, "whether it be good or bad" (2 Corinthians 5:10). We must deduce from this that there is no contradiction between Paul's doctrine of justification and his conception of the judgment of God; and that being declared righteous so as to escape the wrath of God (Romans 5:9; 1 Thessalonians 1:10) does not exempt us from rewards or punishment in the last day. In other words, there must be a righteous judgment *among the very ones* who have been arrayed in Christ's righteousness. As Peter said, "judgment must begin at the house of God" (1 Peter 4:17). This demonstrates once saved, always saved, but equally a judgment among the saved (1 Corinthians 3:13-15). That there is another aspect of the final judgment, namely justice to the unsaved, seems obvious by Peter's other remarks, "What shall the end be of them that obey not the gospel of God? And if the righteous scarcely be saved, where shall the ungodly and the sinner appear?" (1 Peter 4:17-18).

Paul's reference to the judgment seat of Christ affirms the lordship of Jesus over all men. Paul could confidently state to those philosophers at Athens that God "hath appointed a day, in which he will judge the world in righteousness by that man whom he hath ordained; whereof he hath given assurance unto all men, in that he hath raised him from the dead" (Acts 17:31). "Wherefore God also hath highly exalted him, and given him a name which is above every name: that at the name of Jesus every knee should bow, of things in heaven, and things in earth, and things under the earth; and that every tongue should confess that Jesus Christ is Lord, to the glory of God the Father" (Philippians 2:9-11). "We shall all stand before the judgment seat of Christ. For it is written, As I live, saith the Lord, every knee shall bow to me, and every tongue shall confess to God" (Romans 14:10-11). However, the references to the judgment seat of Christ are given to us not only to affirm the lordship of Jesus, but also that it should have a direct effect on the way we live our lives now. Paul said, "But why dost thou judge thy brother? or why dost thou set at nought thy brother? for we shall all stand before the judgment seat of Christ" (Romans 14:10). This shows that if we offend our brother or sister it will come out at the judgment. It will do no good, says Paul, to offend your brother. You may get away with it now but you will not get away with it then. This is why he could say, "Therefore judge nothing before the time, until the Lord come, who both will bring to light the hidden things of darkness, and will make manifest the counsels of the hearts: and then shall every man have praise of God" (1 Corinthians 4:5).

When we realise that the judgment seat of Christ will be an open affair, a time when "the decks are cleared," when the total truth of all things will be revealed, such cannot but have an effect on us now. After all, if it is true that "there is nothing covered, that shall not be revealed; neither hid, that shall not be known" (Luke 12:2), it is going to make us decidedly more careful in all we say and do. Jesus also said, "But I say unto you, That every idle word that men shall speak, they shall give account thereof in the day of judgment" (Matthew 12:36). This is frightening. But we have been warned. This is why Paul could say, "For if we would judge ourselves, we should not be judged" (1 Corinthians 11:31). In other words, if we repent now, we will not be chastened later.

For the judgment seat of Christ will for some be that most extreme form of chastening to which I alluded in the previous chapter. Many of us say to ourselves, "I don't mind what God reveals to me at the judgment because He already knows my heart now." In other words, we fancy that at the judgment we will be shielded from the horror of public awareness of our sin. Not so. What will make that day of days a most terrible event will be two major things: seeing God's own grievance with us and having others see it as well. It is the aura of public opinion that shapes so many of our decisions and protects us from many pitfalls. But when I know that on that day God will "bring to light the hidden things of darkness, and will make manifest the counsels of the heart" (1 Corinthians 4:5), I will begin *now* to put things right. If I have a grudge against you, or if I know that I have hurt you - and I also know that it is only a matter of time when the truth will come out - I would be foolish not to get things right with you immediately.

What an embarrassment that Nathan came to David and said, "Thou art the man" (2 Samuel 12:7). But had it not come out then, it would have come out at the judgment. What a wonderful mercy it was to David that it came out then! "Wherefore doth a living man complain, a man for the punishment for his sins?" (Lamentations 3:39). This is why we should rejoice at each and every chastening of God in the here and now. It means that we will not be dealt with openly on that final day - unless, of course, we show contempt for His chastening now and do not walk in the light. "For if we would judge ourselves, we should not be judged (1 Corinthians 11:31). However painful it might be for me to sort things out with you if I have hurt you, it is far better to do it now than have God "bring to light" all that is true then. I am only fooling myself if I harbour a deep hurt, gossip, say something that will undermine another's reputation or influence, or whatever. It is only a matter of time before the whole truth will be revealed. "Therefore whatsoever ye have spoken in darkness shall be heard in the light; and that which ye have spoken in the ear in closets shall be proclaimed upon the housetops" (Luke 12:3).

I am sure you would agree that if one became convinced of this it would have an effect on one's own life. Indeed, that is one of the reasons we have these very statements in the New Testament about the judgment. This is why Paul's reference to it in Romans 14:10 was in the context of the searching questions, "Why dost thou judge thy brother? or why dost thou *set at nought* thy brother?" Have you hurt another? Have you walked over another and you knew in your heart that what you did was wrong? But you thought, "Nobody will ever know." But they will - everybody will.

I cannot imagine a more awesome scene than the Judgment Seat of Christ. I confess that it frightens me. Do not be surprised if there is actually weeping, wailing, and gnashing of teeth *among the saved* who stand before the Lord in that day of days. Martin Luther reportedly claimed he would have three surprises in heaven: that some would be there he didn't expect to see, that some would be missing that he thought would be there, and that he was there himself. But if I may slightly paraphrase Luther, I would say this: I expect to see some "saved by fire" (1 Corinthians 3:15) that I thought would have "an abundant entrance" (2 Peter 1:11). I expect to see some having an "abundant entrance" that I would not have thought to be particularly faithful and obedient to the Lord here below. But, the surprise of surprises (may it be so) is that I myself should not be saved "so as by fire."

Justification by faith alone, then, provides us with forgiveness for our sins and shields us from the everlasting wrath of God in hell (Romans 5:9; 1 Thessalonians 5:9). Moreover, nothing shall separate us from the love of Christ (Romans 8:35). Indeed, our eternal salvation is in no way whatever conditioned by our performance. "For by grace are ye saved [Gr. - "are you being saved"] through faith; and that not of yourselves: it is the gift of God: not of works, lest any man should boast" (Ephesians 2:8-9). Once saved, always saved.

But the same apostle Paul went to great pains to show us that we must "all" stand before the judgment seat of Christ and "give an account" (Romans 14:12). The imputed righteousness of Christ spares us God's ever-lasting wrath but not the responsibility to keep Christ's commands. That is one chief purpose of the judgment seat of Christ. Why do we have the Sermon on the Mount? Why do we have the teachings of Jesus? They are given to show us how to enjoy the kingdom of God. Loss of inheritance in heaven below means the loss of reward in heaven above. Thus when Paul brings in the judgment seat of Christ, a concept which pulls together a considerable number of verses in the Bible, he is showing in what sense our obedience *does* count for something after all.

This is why Peter could say, "And if ye call on the Father, who without respect of persons judgeth according to every man's work, *pass the time of your sojourning here in fear*" (1 Peter 1:17). It is not until a man is converted that he can begin to produce works that please God. This is why the order of salvation is so important. Works done before conversion are of no value. In fact they can be positively damaging, for they play into man's self-righteous nature, leading him to think that he can be saved by his works.

But there is also a sense in which works after conversion can be damaging. Why? The only work after conversion that has any value at all is "faith which worketh by love" (Galatians 5:6). Any other work can play into our self-righteous nature and deceive us into thinking we are pleasing God by nothing but common morality. That which morality cannot produce in a million years is faith that works by love. It is precisely that which the law cannot produce. The Galatians were so foolish that they imagined that the works of the law brought them into added favour with God. "Are ye so foolish? having begun in the Spirit, are ye now made perfect by the flesh?" (Galatians 3:3). The consequence was that these Galatians made Christ of "no effect." They were *cut off* from Christ in that miserable state. "Christ is become of no effect unto you, whosoever of you are justified by the law; ye are fallen from grace" (Galatians 5:4). It was not grace they were depending on at that particular moment, it was their works. Fortunately for them the promise by the faith of Christ could not be undone. That Paul believed these same people were saved is affirmed by him soon afterwards, "I have confidence in you through the Lord, that ye will be none otherwise minded" (Galatians 5:10). He believed his epistle would wake them up.

What Paul means by faith working by love is exactly what James means by "justification by works" (James 2:21). One of the sadder moments in church history is Luther's utterance that the epistle of James was "an epistle of straw." Luther became so enamoured with his discovery of justification by faith alone that he found himself in an entrenched position that was sometimes counter-productive. What a pity that Luther did not see what a friend he had in James. James's own doctrine of imputed righteousness is as intact as anything Paul taught. "Abraham believed God, and it was imputed unto him for righteousness" (James 2:23).

James's statement about being justified by works was not with reference to salvation at all; it referred to an indiscriminate love for all men. The context is this: James's hearers had slipped back into a fleshly tendency that is in all of us - to become respecters of persons. The people had become partial in their attitude when it came to evangelistic outreach. They were in danger of becoming nothing but a middle-class, religious country club. When a man with a gold ring and goodly apparel walked into their assembly, he received the royal treatment (James 2:2-3). But the poor man was quickly put in his place. "Ye have despised the poor" (James 2:6). The poor became the underlying concern of James.

The Christians James was addressing were like so many of us who would rather say "God bless you" than get personally involved. They thought they were carrying out their pious duty by saying "God bless you" to the man who was hungry and nearly freezing to death. In other words, saying "God bless you" is faith, yes, but "what good does it do?" asks James. To say to a starving, freezing man, "Depart in peace, be ye warmed and filled" is sheer mockery, argues James. What is more; it is "faith alone" to talk like that to the hungry beggar! But if "ye give them not those things which are needful to the body; what doth it profit? Even so faith, if it hath not works, is dead, being alone" (James 2:16-17).

I believe this explains that difficult verse, "What doth it profit, my brethren, though a man say he hath faith, and have not works? can faith save him?" (James 2:14). Our natural reaction to James 2:14 is almost always to assume that James is questioning whether the man who has faith without works can be saved. "Can faith save him?" But this is in fact a hasty interpretation. James is not raising that issue at all. He is not questioning whether we can be saved without works (or he could be opposing Paul), but whether our "faith alone" does anybody else any good. The "him" of James 2:14 is no

171

doubt the same "poor man" of James 2:6. The destitute "brother or sister" of the following verse also confirms that the "him" of verse 14 was someone other than the person who has "faith only."*

But what is even more likely to be overlooked in this passage is that James says all this in the context of the judgment. In warning his hearers of the danger of being a respecter of persons (James 2:9) he added, "So speak ye, and so do, as they that shall be judged by the law of liberty. For he shall have *judgement without mercy*, that hath shewed no mercy; and mercy rejoiceth against judgment" (James 2:12-13). Jesus said that they shall say in that day, "Lord, when saw we thee an hungred, or athirst, or a stranger, or naked, or sick, or in prison, and did not minister unto thee?" (Matthew 25:44).

I think of the words of the great C. T. Studd: "If Jesus Christ be God and died for me, then no sacrifice can be too great for me to make for Him." Paul's sacrifice was partly that he took no remuneration from the people of Corinth. The remarkable paradox, however, is that such a sacrifice is never without reward. "If I do this thing willingly, I have a reward . . . What is my reward then? Verily that, when I preach the gospel, I may make the gospel of Christ without charge, that I abuse not my power in the gospel" (1 Corinthians 9:17-18). Of course this was sacrifice. But Paul knew he could not do this unrewarded. He had virtually the same vision Moses had, esteeming the reproach of Christ greater riches than the treasures in Egypt: "for he had respect unto the recompense of the reward" (Hebrews 11:26).

* See Appendix 1

Thus Paul disclosed that no sacrifice can bring self-pity. "Every man that striveth for the mastery is temperate in all things. Now they do it to obtain a corruptible crown; but we an incorruptible (1 Corinthians 9:25). So determined was Paul to receive this crown that he confessed, "I keep under my body, and bring it into subjection: lest that by any means, when I have preached to others, I myself should be a castaway" (l Corinthians 9:27). This verse has been regarded by some as referring to salvation By "castaway" Paul did not mean losing his salvation. He feared losing the "crown," the "reward." The context makes this clear. Paul feared being "rejected" or set aside after all the preaching he had done. It is a fact that such a thing has happened to many a great man

It will now be necessary to look carefully at a Greek word, *adokimos*. It is translated "castaway" in 1 Corinthians 9:27; "reprobate" in 2 Corinthians 13:5-7; "rejected" in Hebrews 6:8. It means "tested, but not approved The letter a in *adokimas* is known in Greek grammar as the alpha primitive, which gives the word the opposite meaning. For example, *dokimos* means "tested, and approved." The verbal form is *dokimazo* which means "to prove by trial". It is used in James 1:12: "Blessed is the man that endureth temptation: for when he is *tried*, he shall receive the dawn of life, which the Lord hath promised to them that love him." In other words, the man who endures temptation "passes the test" and will receive a crown. Not to pass the test is to be *adokimos* - "castaway," rejected. *Adokmos* is often used to refer to the believer and has considerable significance for this study on the Judgement Seat of Christ.

In 2 Corinthians 13:5-7, Paul takes up with them the question of accreditation and expresses himself to the effect that it matters little to him whether he himself seems to be "approved" so long as they show themselves approved by Jesus Christ being manifest in them. Paul is not turning on them at the last moment and raising the question whether or not they are even saved (how often people quote 2 Corinthians 13:5 out of context); he challenges them to prove their own worth in the light of his apostleship being questioned. The Greek does not read, "Examine yourselves *to see* if you are in the faith"; it is rather, "Examine yourselves if you *are* in the faith." As they were seeking a proof of Christ speaking through Paul (2 Corinthians 13:3), Paul turns on them and asks them to prove that Christ is speaking through them. Thus he says that Jesus Christ is speaking in them unless they have failed the test (2 Corinthians 13:5). The contrast is not that of being saved or lost, but whether or not, as saved people, Christ is openly manifest in them.

This kind of testing is not exactly the same thing as being "tried by fire" at the judgment seat of Christ, although the notion of being proved by testing is not completely unrelated. There is a certain test that will prove whether or not Christ is speaking through us. This test does not await the judgment seat of Christ, but one cannot but notice how important it is to be so utterly yielded to the Lord that we know He is speaking through us. It is this kind of obedience that will be tried on the last day. Indeed, on that day "every man's work shall be made manifest: for the day shall declare it, because it shall be revealed by fire; and the fire shall try *[dokimasei]* every man's work of what sort it is" (1 Corinthians 3:13). Fire will determine whether or not one is approved or rejected. The fire shall try every man's work. It is here that the matter of rewards emerges. "If any man's work abide which he hath built thereupon, he shall receive a reward" (1 Corinthians 3:14). This refers primarily to the minister of the gospel, as we shall see below, but it equally embraces all men - whatever their calling. A man's work may be "burned." If it is, says Paul, he shall suffer loss - obviously loss of reward; "but he himself shall be saved; yet so as by fire" (1 Corinthians 3:15). Once saved, always saved.

It is this matter of reward that partly lay behind the concern of the writer of the epistle to the Hebrews. The phrase "recompense of reward" appears three times in the epistle (Hebrews 2:2, 10:35; 11:26). These Hebrew Christians were not in danger of rejecting but neglecting "so great salvation" (Hebrews 2:3). The rejection of salvation would mean eternal punishment in hell; the neglecting of it means a "just recompense of reward" (Hebrews 2:2) at the Judgment Seat of Christ. Indeed, the writer uses the analogy of fire the same as that in 1 Corinthians 3:13-15. In Hebrews 6:8 we find the words "rejected" *(adokimos)* and "burned"; Hebrews 10:27 warns of judgment and "fiery" indignation. The theme of judgment is clear in this epistle. "As it is appointed unto men once to die, but after this the judgment" (Hebrews 9:27).

The Judgment Seat of Christ I believe provides the explanation of those two very difficult passages - Hebrews 6:4-6 and Hebrews 10:26-31. Some who read these lines will be aware of the long controversy over the interpretation of these two passages. One would need to write a book this size to do full justice to either passage! Therefore it would be a bit optimistic to hope to convince the reader here of their final meaning. I simply put forward the view that the "falling away" (Hebrews 6:6) or "sinning wilfully" (Hebrews 10:26) refers not to losing salvation but one's reward at the judgment seat of Christ. The Arminians have looked on Hebrews 6:4-6 as proof enough that one can lose one's salvation. However, it is not surprising that the Arminians say little more about Hebrews 6:4-6, because it clearly says that those who fall away cannot be renewed "again unto repentance." I have yet to meet the first Arminian who really believes that. Indeed they are found urging men and women to "come back to the Lord," to be "reclaimed" or "restored." That flies in the face of Hebrews 6:6.

Calvinists generally have looked at Hebrews 6:4-6 as a description of unregenerated people. Following John Owen, the great Puritan theologian, it is argued that those in Hebrews 6:4-6 were illuminated , not regenerated. In other words, they never were saved. For a long time I confess that I took this line, accepting Owen and others uncritically, for it seemed the best way to refute Arminianism. I think I was a bit hasty and too anxious to find ammunition with which to argue rather than to let God's word speak for itself.

C. H. Spurgeon believed those described in Hebrews 6:4-6 were obviously saved but the situation posed was hypothetical. Spurgeon built his whole case on the little word *if* - "if they shall fall away" (Hebrews 6:6). Spurgeon claimed it had never happened yet. Unfortunately,

Spurgeon didn't know Greek and he was unaware that there is no *if* in the Greek at all. As a matter of fact those described in Hebrews 6:4-6 had already fallen away. *Parapesontas* is an aorist participle, which is to be translated either as those who "fell away" or those "having fallen away." Their fall was a fact. How they fell or what sin or sins they committed we are not told, neither do we know why the writer was convinced these particular persons could not be renewed again to repentance. It should be noted that it was *repentance* to which they could not be restored. Not salvation. Repentance. So with Esau who "found no place of repentance, though he sought it carefully with tears" (Hebrews 12:17). Luther believed that Esau himself was saved in the end. That one is not restored to repentance, then, does not mean one is not saved. It is to become what Paul calls a "castaway" (1 Corinthians 9:27).

One reason I believe those in Hebrews 6:4-6 were saved is this. It seems to me that the writer is actually labouring to show that they were saved. Why bother to list such descriptions - "enlightened," "tasted of the heavenly gift," "made partakers of the Holy Ghost," "tasted the good word of God, and the powers of the world to come" (Hebrews 6:4-5)? These Hebrew Christians whom the writer addresses were discouraged enough already. Had the writer meant to say that those who fell away were not even saved, although he goes into such detail to show "non-Christian graces," it would almost be demoralising to discouraged Christians. I believe he was showing that such people were saved but had nothing to "accompany" their salvation - in other words, no reward. Thus the writer could say to the rest, "But, beloved, we are persuaded better things of *you*, and things that *accompany* salvation, though we thus speak" (Hebrews 6:9)*.

What those who fell away did, then, was to bring the name of Jesus Christ into reproach. They undoubtedly remained too friendly with the world (James 4:4). They possibly began to commit the sins for which they had been forgiven, or as Peter put it, having "forgotten" that they were "purged" from their "old sins" (2 Peter 1:9). They did not fall from salvation but from the level of walking in the light that is conducive to renewed repentance.

Peter went on to warn of the danger of falling from such: "Ye therefore, beloved, seeing ye know these things before, beware lest ye also, being led away with the error of the wicked, fall from your own steadfastness" (2 Peter 3:17). Falling from steadfastness is to become vulnerable to crucifying Christ a second time, putting him to an "open shame" (Hebrews 6:6). The way one puts Jesus back on the cross, then, is to return openly to the very sins Christ died to atone for. This shows contempt for the name of Christ. I can only believe that those who fell away were people who had been warned again and again until, finally, God swore in His wrath concerning them (cf. Hebrews 3:11). They were the thorns and briers - "rejected" (Hebrews 6:8). This coheres with Jesus' words, "If a man abide not in me, he is cast forth as a branch, and is withered; and men gather them, and cast them into the fire, and they are burned" (John 15:6; cf. Matthew 7:19). So with those who crucified Christ afresh, "whose end is to be burned" (He-

* See Appendix 2

178

brews 6:8). Jesus clearly said, "Every branch in me that beareth not fruit he taketh away" John 15:2). This is the place of "no repentance." That is the issue: They reached the place where God simply rejected them for heaven below and any reward in heaven above. They would be saved by fire (1 Corinthians 3:15).

Hebrews 10:26-31 teaches exactly the same thing. Those who sinned wilfully were those who spurned any warning. knowing that God is "slow to anger" (Psalm 103:8), one can be sure that such people were not merely those suddenly "overtaken in a fault" (Galatians 6:1). We've all been in that state at one time or another. I should think that those who sinned wilfully according to Hebrews 10:26 would be like Jonah if he had not obeyed when God came "the second time" (Jonah 3:1). I cannot believe that sinning wilfully according to Hebrews 10:26 is anything less than continued rebellion against Christ after repeated warnings. This is surely why the writer could be sure of those in Hebrews 6:4-6 he had knowledge of the situation.

It follows that if "we" sin wilfully, "there remaineth no more sacrifice for sins" (Hebrews 10:26). In other words, the blood of Jesus Christ will not cleanse from all sin because "sinning wilfully" is hardly walking in the light (cf. 1 John 1:7). Thus to show contempt for the light of God is to forfeit the cleansing blood of Christ. He was "purged from his old sins," yes. But by not giving all diligence to add to our faith virtue, and to virtue knowledge, and to knowledge temperance (2 Peter 1:5f) such a person shows himself "blind, and cannot see afar off" (2 Peter 1:9). He was purged from his old sins. Once saved, always saved. But there will be no "abundant entrance" into Christ's "everlasting kingdom" (2 Peter 1:11). For the "sacrifice for sins" has been taken away so that such sins will stare him in the face at the judgment. All that remains is "a certain fearful looking for of judgment and fiery indignation" (Hebrews 10:27).

The writer of the epistle to the Hebrews alludes to the two-fold application of the blood of Christ that is to be seen throughout the New Testament. There is the primary application of Christ's blood, namely the forgiveness of sins "that are past" (Romans 3:25). It is this application of Christ's blood that also clothes us with the righteousness of Christ. The writer of Hebrews expresses this in these words: "Their sins and their iniquities will I remember no more" (Hebrews 8:12; 10:17). That is what he means by Christ obtaining an "eternal redemption for us" (Hebrews 9:12), and it is why this one offering for sin "hath perfected for ever them that are sanctified" (Hebrews 10:14). Those that are sanctified (Gr. - "set apart from common use") are those who have been set apart by the blood of Christ - the ones sanctified are *passive* - and are perfected forever, "perfected for all time" (NASB).

This is not an inward perfection but rather a declaration of their eternal standing. The Greek word means "completed" or "finished." Thus we are "sanctified through the offering of the body of Jesus Christ once for all" (Hebrews 10:10). It is not a sanctification by walking in the light in this case, but of God's separating us from our sins by Christ's offering "once for all." This refers to our eternal redemption - once saved, always saved.

But there is a forgiveness of sins that is the result of

our walking in the light. When Jesus said, "If ye forgive not men their trespasses, neither will your Father forgive your trespasses" (Matthew 6:15). He was not referring to whether or not we will be eternally saved. Not at all. This refers to a daily cleansing of Christ's blood. Hence there is an application of the blood of Christ which has direct relevance to our daily lives.

The context of Hebrews 10:26 shows that this particular application of Christ's blood would be forfeited if one continued in one's rebellion against God's will after repeated warnings. Hebrews 10:19-25 shows the relevance of Christ's blood for the way we actually live and it concludes with a reference to exhorting each other. "Not forsaking the assembling of ourselves together, as the manner of some is; but exhorting one another: and so much the more, as ye see the day approaching (Hebrews 10:25). The sinning wilfully (Hebrews 10:26) obviously refers to doing so in the face of such exhortations from fellow believers. The melancholy consequence is that there remains "no sacrifice for sins," for those sins will haunt one at the Judgment Seat of Christ (Hebrews 10:26).

Those people who had sinned like that were actually "sanctified" by the "blood of the covenant" (Hebrews 10:29). That is simply one more bit of evidence showing that we are talking about truly saved people. The problem with them was that they regarded such a covenant as "an unholy thing" by the way they themselves lived. They consequently would fall into the hands of the living God (Hebrews 10:31). The final proof that these people were saved is this: "the Lord shall judge *his people*" (Hebrews 10:30). This is a clear reference to saved people. There is, of course, a judgment for all men. But that aspect of judgment to which the writer of the epistle to the Hebrews is referring is what Paul calls the judgment seat of Christ. "We" shall all stand before it, says Paul (2 Corinthians 5:10). And now the writer of Hebrews includes himself, "If we sin wilfully." I'm sure that he believed he was saved - even as Paul did when he was afraid of being a "castaway" (1 Corinthians 9:27). The meaning I believe is exactly the same. The writer poses the same possibility as that of Paul in 1 Corinthians 3:15 - to be saved "so as by fire."

It was in the context of the Christian ministry that Paul introduced the judgment seat of Christ as he did in 1 Corinthians 3. It was a warning to us ministers to beware how we build on the foundation which is Christ (1 Corinthians 3:10-11). But, whereas it was the ministry that immediately precipitated the discussion, it is not the ministry only that will be judged on the last day. Far from it! This is partly why Paul went straight into this solemn warning: "Know ye not that ye are the temple of God, and that the Spirit of God dwelleth in you? If any man defile the temple of God, him shall God destroy; for the temple of God is holy, which temple ye are" (1 Corinthians 3:16-17). There may be more than one way to "defile" the temple of the Holy Spirit, but the way Paul specifically mentions is by sexual sin (cf. 1 Corinthians 6:18-20). Therefore let no one think that it is only the ministry that will be judged, or that the judgment seat of Christ will be merely a sorting out of the faithfulness of ministers to their congregations.

For Paul says "if any man" build upon Christ "gold, silver, precious stones, wood, hay, stubble; every man's work shall be made manifest: for the day shall declare it, because it shall be revealed by fire; and the fire shall try *every* man's work of what sort it is" (l Corinthians 3:12-13). Imagine a metal tray on which are scattered gold, silver, precious stones, wood, hay, stubble. Sprinkle petrol over these, strike a match and what will you find minutes later? Gold, silver, precious stones.

It would seem that gold, silver and precious stones would be analogous to "faith which worketh by love" (Galatians 5:6).The wood, hay, and stubble would be analogous to any work of the flesh - all self-righteousness and disobedience. To the one who through much tribulation enters the kingdom of God (Acts 14:22), walks in the light (1 John 1:7), keeps his body under subjection (1 Corinthians 9:27), and "loves Christ's appearing" (2 Timothy 4:8) there will be a prize, a crown, a reward. To the one who "sows to the flesh" (Galatians 6:8), "defiles the temple of the Holy Spirit" (l Corinthians 3:17), makes friends of the world (James 4:4), and thus brings Christ's glorious name into disrepute (Hebrews 6:6) there will be no prize, no crown, no reward. "He shall suffer loss: but he himself shall be saved; yet so as by fire" (l Corinthians 3:15).

This I believe to be the apostle's teaching particularly and that of the New Testament generally. Once *saved*, always *saved*. Some will be "saved so as by fire." But they will be saved. They are saved because they confessed Jesus as the Lord and believed in their hearts that God raised Him from the dead. They are saved by sheer grace - by the imputed righteousness of Jesus Christ. But wearing that glorious robe, according to the apostle, does not exempt one from standing before Christ and giving account of the "things done in the body" (2 Corinthians 5:10). Moreover, wearing that glorious robe does not remove the possibility of a reward that "accompanies" salvation (Hebrews 6:9). Paul wanted that reward. He wanted it very much indeed. For Paul knew that eternity lasts a long time. Paul did not like the idea of being *rewardless* throughout eternity.

Some say, "I'll just be glad to be saved." Not Paul. He wanted that reward. Jesus said, "And, behold, I come quickly; and my reward is with me, to give every man according as his work shall be" (Revelation 22:12).

10

The Weak, The Carnal, And The Counterfeit

The teachings of Jesus, especially the parables, often envisage three categories of people who would make up the visible church: the mature Christian, the immature Christian, and the counterfeit. The first two are saved, but the counterfeit is not saved. The obvious difficulty is to determine the difference between the immature Christian, who is just as saved as the mature Christian, and the counterfeit, who, in this case, has never been saved. The origin and destiny of the counterfeit was described by Jesus. "Every plant, which my heavenly Father *hath not planted*, shall be rooted up" (Matthew 15:13).

The problem before us is complex. For example, a true Christian can fall into sin and appear to be the opposite of what he should be; the counterfeit can temporarily flourish and make people think he is a Christian. Thus, the real Christian who falls into sin is often hastily judged as an unsaved hypocrite, and the real phony will sometimes go undetected for a while by sincere Christians.

There are two sorts of counterfeits: benign and malignant. Jesus deals with the benign counterfeit in the parable of the sower. Such people intend no harm to the church, neither is there reason to think that such people may not eventually be truly converted. However, the malignant counterfeits are otherwise: they intend harm to the Christian faith and the Bible does not give us hope that such will be saved. Peter and Jude particularly deal with the malignant counterfeit: "For there were certain men crept in unawares, who were before of old ordained to this condemnation, ungodly men, turning the grace of our God into lasciviousness, and denying the only Lord God, and our Lord Jesus Christ" (Jude 4; cf. 2 Peter 2:1).

There are also two sorts of immature Christians: weak and carnal. I think such a distinction comes out in a verse like this: "And through thy knowledge shall the weak brother perish, for whom Christ died?" (1 Corinthians 8:11). The one who has just such "knowledge" is not as mature as he pretends; indeed, he is carnal. For such a person, rather than being mature, is insensitive to a weaker Christian. Thus the opposite of weak in this case is not strong, but carnal. It is but one form of immaturity against another.

I would describe the weak Christian as fearful, slow, and over-conscientious. I would describe the carnal as over-confident, careless, and insensitive. Both the weak and the carnal Christian are indeed saved, but each needs pastoral attention. Such pastoral advice for each emerges particularly in the New Testament epistles. And yet even the weak Christian is carnal as distinct from spiritual. But I would have thought that the thrust of the New Testament suggests that the "carnal" Christian is so nicknamed because of an inexcusable immaturity - he should be much further along than he is.

The mature Christian will surely avoid two extremes. At one end is the presumption that anybody who makes a "decision" for Christ is saved. This flies in the face of the parable of the sower in which Jesus clearly described the seed which fell by the wayside. I would call them innocent counterfeits. "Those by the wayside are they that hear; then cometh the devil, and taketh away the word out of their hearts, *lest they should believe and be saved*" (Luke 8:12). Nothing could be plainer than that. This shows that some would indeed "hear," and that more than mere "listening" took place is obvious because the devil took away "the word out of their hearts." The heart is the seat of faith. It would seem that the word did just reach the heart but that it came short of being effectual. This would seem to describe those who, for whatever reason, prematurely make a profession of faith. Perhaps they say, "I believe." Perhaps they even pray to receive Christ or make a public profession of faith. It is not the task of this chapter to unravel all the ingredients of unbelief that can lie behind a false profession. I only know that Jesus anticipated this sort of thing in the church or He would not have given us the parable of the sower.

The purpose of this chapter is not to cause any sincere Christian to question his salvation. I simply say to the reader, you know whether in your heart of hearts your trust is in Jesus' death on the cross, that you believe He is the Son of God and was raised from the dead. You know whether or not this is the very foundation of your faith. If it is, you may know that you are saved - eternally

187

saved. This chapter is written in order to bring to bear certain biblical passages which are used to refute the general thesis of this book.

The mature Christian will avoid the other extreme - those who cannot bear the thought of someone being saved who has not lived a consistent godly life. Or to use the phrase found in the parable of the vineyard, there are those who resent some who will be granted entrance into heaven, because they have not "borne the burden and heat of the day" (Matthew 20:12).

It is the older - but not necessarily mature Christian, often the more faithful church member, who is prone to sound an awful lot like those envious workers in the vineyard.

All of us must be careful here. The easiest thing in the world is to dismiss a particular person as "not saved" if he is not theologically sharp or if his perseverance in sainthood is doubtful. The tendency for some is, as it were, to "raise the standard" of entrance into the faith which unchristianises those who do not come up to "standard." The "standard" is always the equivalent of the burden we are bearing! But to resent the disobedient one who may be "saved so as by fire" (1 Corinthians 3:15) may betray that we too will be saved so as by fire. For our self-righteousness and jealousy is as obnoxious in God's sight as another's lack of responsibility may be in ours.-

Jesus said, "Follow me, and I will make you fishers of men" (Matthew 4:19). If you wanted to be strict about this, you might say that any follower of Jesus will be a soul winner and if he is not a soul winner he is not a follower of Jesus. I am not trying to make such a case

188

here. But I often use this with people who are so hasty to question whether or not a person is truly saved just because he is not always very obedient. For it has been my observation that precious few who are so quick to question another's conversion are themselves soul winners. These people who think a "carnal" Christian cannot really be a Christian usually don't appreciate the idea that being a "fisher of men" is a test whether or not a person is saved. It is of course no test at all, but many of us tend to make the "standard" at roughly the same level *we* are at home with - even if we are not soul winners or tithers!

Whether we like it or not there is such a thing as a carnal Christian. The word *carnal* comes from a Greek word that simply means "fleshly." It is most certainly not the way the writers of the New Testament envisage how the Christian life ought to be lived. "For to be carnally minded is death; but to be spiritually minded is life and peace" (Romans 8:6).

Paul warned the Galatians that they had reverted to the "flesh" (Galatians 3:3) and that sowing to the flesh would result in "corruption" (Galatians 6:8). Some of the Corinthians, whom Paul plainly called "carnal" (1 Corinthians 3:3), were not surprisingly a demonstration of all that can happen to Christians who choose to live in the flesh. Paul said, "If ye live after the flesh, ye shall die" (Romans 8:13). I am sure that the "dying" is to be contrasted with the quality of life that is "life everlasting" (Galatians 6:8), but the literal physical implications should not be overlooked. "For this cause many are weak and sickly among you, and many sleep" (1 Corinthians 11:30). "Sin, when it is finished, bringeth forth death" (James 1:15). James implied that some illnesses are traceable to sin (James 5:15).

The Hebrew Christians, at least some of them, seem to have been little more mature than the Corinthians (Hebrews 5:12ff).

The great Charles Hodge when commenting on 1 Corinthians 3:1 was bold enough to say that Paul is speaking of "one class of Christians as distinguished from another." Therefore, "when we predicate spirituality to a Christian as compared to other Christians, we mean that he is eminently spiritual." The thesis of this book is open to the charge that there are two "classes" of Christian-those who will have a reward and those who will not. But it is surely unrealistic to shut our eyes to the fact that some Christians are more (or less) spiritual than others. I admit that I am a bit uneasy with the idea of a "class" that is superior or inferior in spirituality, but in the end we are faced with this matter and I know of no way to get around it if we honestly examine all relevant passages. When Paul says, "ye are yet carnal" (1 Corinthians 3:3), he clearly hoped they would soon move beyond that state, and the implication in the same chapter follows that, if they remain carnal, they will be saved "so as by fire" (1 Corinthians 3:15). But they were saved nonetheless.

However, it is equally true that not all who make a profession of faith are saved. There are actually two kinds of counterfeit: the previously mentioned innocent, but also the malicious. It is therefore fair to say that the only explanation for either is that they were never saved in the first place. We have a number of passages in the New Testament that will bear this out - those whom the Father "hath not planted" (Matthew 15:13). John put it like this: "They went out from us, but they were not of us; for if they had been of us, they would no doubt have continued with us; but they went out, that they might be made manifest that they were not all of us" (1 John 2:19).

John was referring to those previously mentioned Gnostics. They had seduced John's "little children" (1 John 2:26). The earmark of these Gnostics was a denial that Jesus is come in the flesh (i.e., Jesus is God). A Gostic could not bring himself to say " Jesus is God." They were also known for their gross immorality (2 Peter 2:14). Fortunately John could report their exodus from the community he was addressing (probably Ephesus). But not all Christian communities were so fortunate. Both Jude and 2 Peter deal with the matter of Gnosticism, which seemed to be rampant. There is a portion of 2 Peter that reads like Jude almost verbatim (cf. 2 Peter 2:10-19 and Jude 8-16). We may, therefore, safely assume that the two books refer to the same people.

This is important. For Jude tells us that they did not come into the faith as genuine believers. They got into the fellowship of the church and they managed to make some sort of profession of faith too. But Jude plainly says that they "wormed their way in" (Jude 4, NEB). For there are certain men *crept* in unawares". who were before of old ordained to this condemnation, ungodly men, turning the grace of our God into lasciviousness, and denying the only Lord God, and our Lord Jesus Christ" (Jude 4). I don't think anything can be plainer than this: these people were simply *not saved*.

But of the very same people Peter said, "For it had been better for them not to have known the way of righteousness, than, after they have known it, to turn from the holy commandment delivered unto them" (2 Peter 2:21). Because of this statement, as well as the one preceding it, some have hastily concluded some people can lose their salvation. "For if after they have escaped the pollutions of the world through the knowledge of the Lord and Saviour Jesus Christ, they are again entangled therein, and overcome, the latter end is worse with them than the beginning" (2 Peter 2:20). But the preceding verses in 2 Peter 2:10-19 show beyond any doubt that they are the exact same people Jude was describing. Jude clearly tells us they were never saved in the first place. It is precisely the point John made about Gnostics. "They went out from us, but they were not of us . . . but they went out, that they might be made manifest that they were not all of us" (1 John 2:19).

But why does Peter say they "escaped the pollutions of the world through the knowledge of the Lord and Saviour Jesus Christ" (2 Peter 2:20)? Because the power of Christian fellowship undoubtedly had a temporary effect on them despite their "worming their way in." They simply could not be around true Christian people for very long without being affected by them. Apparently there was a time during which they were not "entangled" in the pollutions of the world. But Peter knew they were never saved for he prophesied of them, "the latter end is worse with them than the beginning" (2 Peter 2:20).

These Gnostics were in much the same position as Judas Iscariot. Jesus knew from the beginning that

Judas was "a devil" (John 6:70). Who can deny that while Judas walked with Jesus and the other eleven disciples he largely escaped the pollutions of the world? But he was never saved. Jesus affirmed this in John 17:12. Judas also "fell" (Acts 1:25) and it ought not to be surprising that some who flourish for a while make their exodus by a great fall. Jesus said of Judas that "it had been good for that man if he had not been born (Matthew 26:24). For those who are within the influence of the godly add to their condemnation, thus showing "it had been better for them not to have known the way of righteousness" (2 Peter 2:21). But people like that were never saved. Jude 4 categorically resolves this.

What these Gnostics lacked was true repentance. It is possible to have "known the way" without repentance. As we said earlier, repentance is the translation of the Greek word *metanoia,* which means "change of mind." It basically means "agreeing with God." It is saying "I was wrong." Such a humble state of mind was alien to these Gnostics. Repentance is a vital ingredient in saving faith. For there is an inherent admission "I was wrong" or "I agree with God" in anyone's true confession. It is true that the apostle Paul did not refer to repentance often, but a "change of mind" is implicit in one's confession in Romans 10:9-10 (cf. Acts 20:21). If one asks, which comes first, faith or repentance, it depends how one defines repentance. If one sticks with its biblical meaning - "change of mind" - then one can only say that they come together. But if one defines repentance, as "turning from every known sin" (as some Puritans were inclined to do), one can see the endless confusion that will emerge if such "repentance" is demanded prior to faith. The result has been doom and gloom, being never quite sure they are saved, owing to a fear they have not repented enough. At any rate, those Gnostics knew the *way* but never did they know *repentance*.

The Gnostics had a shattering effect upon true believers. That was true in the community John addressed (1 John 2:26) and also in that which concerned Jude (12) and Peter (2 Peter 2:14ff). Peter compares the effect they had on the church with the effect Sodom and Gomorrah had on Lot. These Gnostics, whom Peter calls "false prophets" and "false teachers" (2 Peter 2:1), were counterfeit. Lot, however, typifies the carnal Christian. Lot foolishly chose to pitch his tent near Sodom where the men "were wicked and sinners before the Lord exceedingly" (Genesis 13:12-13). Their influence on Lot was predictable and in the end he barely escaped the destruction God sent upon that country (Genesis 19:15-25). And yet Peter calls him " just Lot (Gr. *dikaion* - "righteous" - 2 Peter 2:7). I wonder how many of us would call Lot righteous! Had Peter not said that, it would probably never have entered into our minds to impute this to Lot. But Peter did say it, and that settles it. That also shows the consistency of Paul in calling those Corinthians "carnal" (1 Corinthians 3:3). As Charles Hodge put it, "In like manner we speak of some Christians as worldly or carnal, without intending to deny that they are Christians."

But it is not only counterfeits that can do damage to the church; even a true Christian can hurt his own brother in Christ. "Take heed lest by any means this liberty of yours become a stumbling block to them that are weak" (1 Corinthians 8:9). The particular offence at that time was eating of meats that had been sacrificed to idols. Some Christians did not have that problem, but weak Christians did have it, and it shattered the latter to see any Christians eating meat that had been sacrificed to idols. Thus Paul addressed the carnal Christian. "And through thy knowledge shall the weak brother perish, for whom Christ died?" (1 Corinthians 8:11).

This verse (1 Corinthians 8:11) has been offered as proof that a person can lose his salvation because of the word perish. I must admit that if Paul used the word in the same precise manner that our Lord did in John 3:16, then our case is weakened. It would also mean that a person could lose his soul because he came under the influence of a carnal Christian. I do not believe that is Paul's point. As the Greek word *adokimos* can be used both of a Christian (1 Corinthians 9:27) and a non-Christian (Romans 1:28), so can the Greek word *apollumi* (perish) apply to the opposite of eternal life (John 3:16), but also a temporal place of uselessness. For this word also means "to come to nought" or "to lose." Indeed, our Lord uses this word to describe the one who would not "lose his reward" (Matthew 10:42).

It would not be surprising if this indeed is Paul's meaning in this epistle which emphasises rewards. But apart from that possibility I am sure that it simply means what we today mean by shattered, deeply hurt, or crushed. It is to say that the weaker brother is so shaken by observer a fellow Christian do the "unthinkable" that he is, at least for a while, of no use to the church. It could even mean that the weaker Christian becomes so demoralised that in the end he forfeits any possibility of a reward for himself. This I believe to be the meaning also of the similar statement in Romans 14:15. Merely because such strong terms can be applied to Christians should not lead us to the hasty conclusion that such must not be Christians at all.

I do not think Paul thought younger widows would lose their salvation because they would want to remarry, yet he said, "they will marry; having damnation, because they have cast off their first faith" (1 Timothy 5:11-12). "Damnation" is a strong word in English and therefore one questions the translation also in Romans 14:23; "He that doubteth is damned if he eat, because he eateth not of faith; for whatsoever is not of faith is sin." But the Greek word in both passages is from *krino* which means "to make a distinction between "to exercise judgment upon." The same word is used earlier in the same chapter where it is translated "esteemeth" (Romans 14:5). It is translated " judge" in Matthew 7:1. It is therefore left to the translator's discretion. I do not think many interpreters would say that young widows who remarry will lose their salvation, or that anyone else would lose his salvation should he ever doubt. I believe the meaning in 1 Timothy 5:12 and Romans 14:23 is simply this: such people make themselves liable to being adversely judged by God.

Passages like these reflect the godly concern of the apostle who knows how Satan will drive a wedge in a vulnerable area of a Christian's life. The little foxes "spoil the vines" (Song of Solomon 2:15). It may be a matter such as being offended over a Christian eating meat sacrificed to idols that leads to something extremely serious. What begins as apparently harmless can develop into something grave. If not dealt with in time, Satan can successfully turn it into a major defeat for the Christian.

What Paul cherished was "a good conscience; which some having put away concerning faith have made shipwreck: of whom is Hymenaeus and Alexander; whom I have delivered unto Satan, that they may learn not to blaspheme" (1 Timothy 1:19-20). One keeps a good conscience by watching out for the "little foxes."

We do not know what lay behind the "shipwrecked faith" of Alexander and Hymenaeus. It may have started with something very small. But it became necessary for Paul to deliver them both to Satan. I would have thought that both men were saved or Paul would not have used the same expression as he did for the man in Corinth. We know the man in Corinth was saved. We don't know what the two men had done that was so wicked, but it apparently had not yet come to the notice of the world. When Paul said, "that they may learn not to blaspheme" (1 Timothy 1:20), it may have meant that their sin had not come to the notice of the world so as to bring the name of Christ into reproach. "Alexander the coppersmith [possibly the same Alexander] did me much evil: the Lord reward him according to his works" (2 Timothy 4:14). This further suggests that the "delivering unto Satan" was to hasten death that the spirit may be saved in the day of Christ. The reward "according to his works" apparently refers to the judgment seat of Christ.

Delivering one to Satan seems to be an expression that means more than just excommunication. To deliver one utterly outside the realm of Christ into the realm of

Satan seems to indicate that death - physical death - will not be far away. Some take "destruction of the flesh" (1 Corinthians 5:5) to mean the carnal nature. This was G. Campbell Morgan's view. I rather think that there are sins that hasten the judgment of God upon one. I therefore take this also to be the "sin unto death" (1 John 5:1-6).

The sin unto death is not the same thing as the blasphemy against the Holy Spirit. A Christian cannot commit the blasphemy of the Spirit which is to deny the true person of Jesus Christ in the flesh. No man can say that Jesus is the Lord but by the Holy Ghost (1 Corinthians 12:3). To deny the deity of Jesus is therefore to show contempt for the work of the Spirit, whose function it is to reveal Christ (John 15:26; 16:13-14). Jesus spoke of the blasphemy of the Spirit because some said of Jesus, "He hath an unclean spirit" (Mark 3:2-30). But embodied in the Christian profession of faith is the heart confession that Jesus is Lord (Romans 10:9), which affirms the testimony of the Spirit.

The "sin unto death" is not the blasphemy of the Spirit, then, but the sort of sin which hastens the judgment of God and may result in a "premature" death. It is good to know that "there is a sin not unto death" (1 John 5:17), or none of us would be alive. I am not prepared to say what sin constitutes the sin unto death, but if I am right in attaching it to the scandalous situation in Corinth it would suggest that such a sin must be extremely hazardous for the work of the gospel. This would be why God intervenes in this extreme manner. I am inclined to bring in Ananias and Sapphira in this connection (Acts 5:1-11).

For God has called us unto holiness (1 Thessalonians 4:7). There have always been those who say that how one lives is irrelevant to God. It seems that the Gnostics made that claim. John answers, "Whosoever is born of God doth not commit sin; for his seed remaineth in him: and he cannot sin, because he is born of God" (1 John 3:9). This verse connects to an earlier statement, "If we say that we have fellowship with him, and walk in darkness, we lie, and do not the truth" (1 John 1:6). It refutes the notion that, "God said it is all right for me to do this" even though it transgresses the law. "He that committeth sin is of the devil" (1 John 3:8). This does not mean that anyone who sins is irrevocably destined to be one of Satan's children because one sins, but it shows that the one who goes against the revealed will of God is - at that moment - governed by Satan.

Peter was governed by the devil when He rebuked Jesus for prophesying of His death and resurrection. Jesus said to Peter, "Get thee behind me, Satan" (Matthew 16:23). Whenever we go against God's revealed will, we reveal that we let Satan speak instead of God. You can never sin and claim God as the author of it. It is in this vein that John says the child of God "cannot sin" (1 John 3:9). This does not mean that he is exempt from the possibility (cf. 1 John 2:1), but that there is only one standard of living that God recognises as being congruous with His own nature. There is a sin "not unto death" (1 John 5:17) which shows that a Christian can sin. But if you want to know how serious God is when He says we "cannot" - there is "a sin unto death" (1 John 5:16). It is like when I say to my son or daughter, "You cannot do this." They may want to reason with me, even argue, but if I stick to my guns they know I mean it. That I believe is John's point.

For there is no possibility of fellowship with God apart from "walking in the light" (1 John 1:7). As we saw in an earlier chapter, that is what Paul often calls "inheriting the kingdom of God" and what the writer of Hebrews calls "entering God's rest." For such an inheritance comes to those who continue in the faith. It promises a partaking of Christ that makes Him so real that we would not trade places with the disciples in Galilee!

It is a vital, living realisation of Christ, however, that comes only by perseverance. That is why the writer said, "We are made partakers of Christ, if we hold the beginning of our confidence steadfast unto the end" (Hebrews 3:14). That is not a reference merely to being saved but to a lively partaking of the very person of Jesus that makes Him as real to us by the Spirit as He was to the disciples in the flesh. That is what God's rest is (Matthew 11:29). The writer earlier called it the superstructure upon the foundation, which is Christ, "whose *house* are we, if we hold fast the confidence and the rejoicing of the hope firm unto the end" (Hebrews 3:6). It is building with gold, silver, and precious stones, not wood, hay, and stubble. Such a building, or house, is erected by obedience and perseverance. The result is heaven below - partaking of Christ - and a reward in heaven above. Jesus said, "If ye continue in my word, then are ye my disciples indeed" (John 8:31).

Someone will ask about Matthew 24:13: "He that shall endure to the end, the same shall be saved" (cf. Mark 13:13). I do not believe that *saved* in this place means salvation as we have defined it in this book. Sometimes the word *saved* has a rather different meaning, as in 1 Timothy 2:15: "Notwithstanding she shall be saved in childbearing, if they continue in faith and charity and holiness with sobriety." This refers to the dignity of womanhood being restored in the light of Eve's sin (1 Timothy 2:13-14). I think saved in Matthew 24:13 and Mark 13:13, as well as Matthew 10:22, means a miraculous deliverance after a most severe kind of tribulation and persecution. I think the term saved in these verses is used as in Jeremiah 30:7: "Alas! for that day is great, so that none is like it: it is even the time of Jacob's trouble; but he shall be *saved* out of it."

Thus, in our Lord's warning of an awful ordeal to come, He promised them a victorious escape from the entrapments of severe persecution by "taking no thought" but letting the Spirit speak in them (Matthew 10:19-20). It meant that they were not to turn back though the temptation should be great. It was in a similar context that Jesus said, "Remember Lot's wife" (Luke 17:32) who turned into a pillar of salt by looking back at Sodom (Genesis 19:26). But if one will endure to the end, he will not be hurt at all. "There shall not an hair of your head perish" (Luke 21:18). There is the deliverance that is promised.

I fear I will have left out some verses that will continue to haunt some sincere Christian who may still be afraid he could lose his salvation. But I have tried to provide a consistent biblical framework, which I hope, will enable the reader to go from here and apply the word of God himself. In the end that is what we all must do. As Paul said to Timothy, "Study to shew thyself approved unto God, a workman that needeth not to be ashamed, rightly dividing the word of truth" (2 Timothy 2:15).

The immature Christian is nothing new. It is great consolation that the New Testament writers alluded to him as well (1 Corinthians 3:3; Hebrews 5:12; James 3:10). And was that not the greatest of all spiritual times? We may, therefore, assume that we will always have the "weak" and the "carnal" around. The truth is, we've all been weak, if not carnal, at some stage. How patient God is with us. "The Lord is merciful and gracious, slow to anger, and plenteous in mercy ... For he knoweth our frame; he remembereth that we are dust" (Psalm 103:8,14).

Our goal, however, is to "grow in grace, and in the knowledge of our Lord and Saviour Jesus Christ" (2 Peter 3:18). Such maturity will be known partly by our tolerance of the weak, carnal Christian. For if we cannot bear the thought that a carnal Christian is nonetheless saved, we border on betraying our own carnality!

But it has to be said that not all who initially make a profession of faith in Christ are saved. We must be patient with them as well - but also firm. We do people no favour to grant them hope of being saved merely because they have made some kind of profession of faith. For true faith always included a change of mind - repentance.

In the end we cannot judge the other person. We can only judge ourselves. "If we would judge ourselves, we should not be judged" (1 Corinthians 11:31). You cannot ultimately know whether another is saved. But you can know that you are saved. Never doubt it!

Conclusion

On the very day I first realised that God loved me with an "everlasting love" (Jeremiah 31:3), there came to me with equal force yet another discovery: Jesus Christ was literally praying for me at God's right hand. I had heard of that truth before then, of course, but it was not until October 31, 1955, that it was brought home so plainly and personally to me. What I did not fully grasp at the time was that it is the continual intercession of Christ that ultimately guarantees the eternal salvation of every believer.

The intercessory work of our Lord Jesus Christ is by itself sufficient, indeed absolute, proof that those who once truly believe on Him could not possibly come to perdition. To suggest that once saved, always saved is not true borders on showing contempt for all that Jesus is doing for us in heaven. "I pray for them . . . and none of them is lost, but the son of perdition; that the scripture might be fulfilled" (John 17:9, 12). "Who is he that condemneth? It is Christ that died, yea rather, that is risen again, who is even at the right hand of God, who also maketh intercession for us" (Romans 8:34).

What is Jesus doing at God's right hand? He is praying for us! If you want to know the essential content of our Lord's prayer for us in heaven, read all of John 17. The writer of the epistle to the Hebrews says, "Wherefore he is able also to save them to the uttermost that come unto God by him, seeing he ever liveth to make intercession for them" (Hebrews 7:25). The word uttermost is from the Greek *panteles*, which, when used adverbially (as it is here), means "through all time," or "forever."

The real question is, Does our Lord get His prayers answered? Jesus knew that Peter would betray Him. "Simon, behold, Satan hath desired to have you, that he may sift you as wheat: but I have *prayed for thee, that thy faith fail not:* and when thou art converted, strengthen thy brethren" (Luke 22:31-32). Did the Lord get His prayer answered? Of course He did! Look at Peter from the day of our Lord's resurrection onwards.

In the early seventeenth century, Jacobus Arminius argued that believers could not be lost, "as long as they remain believers," but he implied that if one ceased to believe, one was in danger of forfeiting one's salvation. Arminius's teachings (most have been translated into English) not only reveal a faulty doctrine of justification by faith, but also show virtually no understanding of the power and glory of Christ's intercession at God's right hand.

That is yet another reason we must take the faith of Christ with utmost seriousness. Paul took it so seriously that he said, "I *live* by the faith of the Son of God" (Galatians 2:20). It is ultimately Christ's faith that saves and such faith is not only to be seen in the vicarious life

He lived on earth but also in the quality of His own faith in His very prayer for us at God's right hand. If Christ does not pray to the Father with a perfect faith, there is no hope for any of us. But Paul did not worry about Christ having less than a perfect faith. He knew that Christ's faith was adequate - his faith was in Christ's faith.

A few days after my family and I settled into our new home in London, I drove my son to his new school. He was dreading the thought of entering a new school in a land in which none of us ever dreamed of remaining. It would mean strange surroundings, totally new teachers and children, and my son loathed even getting out of the car. I continued to coax him to go to the playground. He sat still in the car. Then I said, "Son, Daddy will be praying for you *all day long*. Whenever you feel scared, remember that Daddy at that moment is praying for you." His countenance changed to one of great relief. Without my saying another word, he opened the car door and walked to his school without looking back. He knew I meant what I said. He did not trust his own prayers - he was living by mine.

"Neither pray I for these alone, but for them also which shall believe on me through their word . . . that they also, whom thou hast given me, be with me where I am; that they may behold my glory" (John 1;7:20, 24).

Salvation is a free gift (Romans 6:23). If I must know whether or not I am saved by the state of my own faithfulness, it is no gift at all. There could also be boasting. But salvation is "not of works, lest any man should boast" (Ephesians 2:9). And yet we "are his workmanship, created in Christ Jesus unto good works, which God hath before ordained that we should walk in them" (Ephesians 2:10).

This book has sought to show the seriousness of the biblical mandate to holy living and the consequences when one does not live a holy life. The same apostle Paul who articulated the glorious doctrine of justification by faith alone also said, "For we must all appear before the judgment seat of Christ; that everyone may receive the things done in his body, according to that he hath done, whether it be good or bad" (2 Corinthians 5:10).

But once saved, always saved. Some will be saved by fire. I should like to think, however, that this book should impel one to give all diligence to make one's calling and election sure. "For so an entrance shall be ministered unto you abundantly into the everlasting kingdom of our Lord and Saviour Jesus Christ" (2 Peter 1:11).

Were the whole realm of nature mine,
That were an offering far too small;
Love so amazing, so divine,
Demands my soul, my life, my all.

Appendix 1

When 1 first began preaching on James in my present pulpit (a series that lasted two and a half years) I took for granted that the traditional argument concerning James 2:14-26 was adequate: "salvation is by faith alone but saving faith is never alone!" Moreover, I was influenced at first by a modern evangelical commentary that suggested that the book of James was a collection of sermon notes. That gave one a feeling that James was not an orderly epistle but rather a string of beads with no definite arrangement. I soon discovered, however, that that was not the case.

James is an epistle of definite order indeed. The "divers temptations" (trials) of James 1:2 is dealt with directly in James 5:7-12. The "wisdom," which Paul would call "faith which worketh by love" (Galatians 5:6), is dealt with in James 3:13 - 4:17. The "brother of low degree" (James 1:9) continues to be the theme right through chapter 2 and is picked up again in James 5:1-4.

James mainly addressed Hebrew Christians who had gotten off track partly due to problems of class distinction. A chief problem was that many were being discriminate in their evangelism. There were also poor people in the church who were being ruthlessly walked over by the more affluent believers. The latter, clearly, were largely in control. It would also appear that there were believers in that community who were actually employed by fellow Christians, such as being "workers in the field" (James 5:4), who were taken advantage of by "rich" Christians (James 5:1ff).

The object of the epistle of James is twofold: (1) to encourage the godly Christians, many of whom were apparently poor, to dignify the trial God had allowed them to have; and (2) to warn the more worldly Christians, some of whom were obviously rich, to see the danger of impending judgment upon them.

Never once does James question whether the rich - or poor - have been saved. Neither does he admonish them in such a way that should cause them to question whether they have been saved. He never says, for example, "The trouble with you people is that you are not saved." He does not come forward with a plan of salvation; he does not warn them of a false assurance; he does not go over the basis of saving faith. So little is there of this sort of thing that Martin Luther once questioned whether the epistle of James should even be in the canon of Scripture. He thought that it was written by a misguided Jew who did not know what he was talking about.

At best Luther regarded James as "an epistle of straw" and, even as late as a year or so before he died advised that James should not be taught in the University of Wittenberg.

Luther was wrong, of course. Very wrong indeed. Luther betrayed the weakness - to which all of us are vulnerable - of having been entrenched so deeply in a theological position that he became too defensive to look at the matter objectively.

James was not only Luther's friend but held to the doctrine of justification by faith alone as strongly - and clearly - as Paul. I first realised that when we came to James 1:2-21. Faith alone saves. James took that for granted. It was of course helpful that he made this more explicit in James 2:23: "Abraham believed God, and it was imputed unto him for righteousness."

In my opinion the heirs of Luther took Luther too seriously. Many felt they had to show that James was only proving that saved people must have works - to prove that they are truly saved. But the error lies in the assumption that James is talking about the authenticity of the salvation of one who does or does not have works. This was not James's concern at all.

James's concern was the poor - literally, the "poor man" in James 2:6. The Greek word is *ptochon*. It is the accusative singular. It is translated "poor man" in the New American Standard Bible, the Revised Standard Version, the New English Bible, the Phillips, and many others. There is nothing wrong of course in translating *ptochon* simply as "poor" or "the poor" - for James wants to come to the defense of all poor people. But the Greek usage is helpful when we come to see that the "him" in James 2:14 is also in the accusative singular.

This is the thrust of the whole of James 2. The context begins not in 2:1 but in 1:22. Having stated that it is the "engrafted word, which is able to save your souls" he immediately adds: "But be ye doers of the word, and not hearers only, deceiving your own selves." Let us consider that carefully. If James means by "but" that one must be a "doer of the word" in order to ratify saving faith, then it must be said firmly and categorically that James does not believe that salvation is the gift of God by faith *alone*. There must be works. One must "do" or be lost. If the "doing of works" must be joined to the "engrafted word which is able to save," then it is not the word that saves but regeneration plus works.

That of course would be an Arminian interpretation. The Arminians (those who believe that salvation is conditional - based upon faith and continued obedience) are very comfortable in this section of James if indeed the issue James is speaking of is that of the validity of one's own salvation.

The Calvinists also have tended to assume what Arminians (and Luther) assumed, namely, that James is worried whether or not these Hebrew Christians are really going to be saved. If they don't have works, they are not saved: "faith without works is dead" (James 2:20), that is, faith alone cannot save if it is not joined by works. But the traditional Calvinist says, "But wait a minute. James is not saying that it is faith that is joined by works which saves, it is merely that James knows that if there are not works following faith, it shows that it was a spurious faith."

The Calvinist is anxious to show that he most certainly believes that we are justified by faith alone; but should it happen that there is not a corresponding life of good works it was nothing but the "faith of devils" in operation.

That is partly why I stated that I, coming into the reformed tradition from the outside, possibly believe in this teaching more than most Calvinists!

Many Calvinists I meet are almost scared to death of the teaching once saved, always saved. They believe it but are afraid to rest in it; they believe it in theory, but they are afraid of it in practice. Their fear of Antinomianism, I suspect, has unwittingly put them in a bondage they don't know how to throw off. They fear that if people really believe they are saved utterly and entirely by what Jesus did on the cross that they will live lawless lives. Were this precious doctrine to be abused it would set it back indeed. It is committed to our "trust" (1 Timothy 1:11). God puts us on our honour. That is scary - but glorious.

What does James mean by "deceiving your own selves"? He tells us straight away. "For if any be a hearer of the word, and not a doer, he is like unto a man beholding his natural face in a glass (mirror): for he beholdeth himself, and goeth his way, and straightway forgetteth what manner of man he was" (James 1:23-24). James does not say that this man proves to himself he is not saved. James simply says that such a man "immediately forgets what he looks like" (NIV). What does that mean? It means that such a person loses objectivity about himself; he does not truly examine his heart; his sense of discernment vanishes; he loses a keen sense of sin; he cannot see himself as others see him.

We have all done that. We have all been guilty of being hearers of the word and not doers. We look at ourselves in the mirror, decide everything is all right, then go out into the streets and see the poor man, the lost

211

man who needs Jesus—but it doesn't seem to bother us. We prefer to say, "Why doesn't he get a job?" or, "It is his own fault that he is like that." Anything to justify ourselves for not caring for people. I know a person who opposed this teaching when I preached it at Westminster Chapel; he called me an Antinomian but would not even go a mile out of his way to pick up a needy person on the way to church. What startles me is the number of people who insist that one must have works to show he is saved but who themselves have virtually *nothing* of the very works James has in mind! They wish to use James as a basis of "assurance by works" but not the kind of works James has in mind - caring for the poor. I have yet to meet the first person who holds (or preaches) that giving another "those things which are needful to the body" must follow faith to show that it is saving faith indeed. We prefer to be selective in our use of James.

What about the person who *is* a doer not a hearer? "This man shall be blessed in his deed." "He will be blessed in what he does" (NIV). God blesses obedience. It is as simple as that. We obey because we are grateful for that "perfect law that gives freedom" (James 1:25, NIV). Why does it give freedom? Because there are not any conditions attached. Conditions bind. They restrict. They bring bondage. But the gospel brings freedom. It releases a person. What is more, this is precisely the gospel that impels a man to show good works. In my pastoral experience I have discovered that those who believe this gospel the most are those who are the most eager to show good works. Figure that one out! It is a fact. Those who are suspicious of this gospel tend to be passive, introspective, sad. Rarely are they soul winners; rarely do you see them talking to beggars or accepting poor people - not to mention inviting them for a meal.

Now to James 2:1. Those Hebrew Christians had become respecters of persons. They wanted to turn Christianity into a middle-class religion. They determined to do that by being discriminate in their evangelism, that is, being selective in whom they witnessed to. Thus if a person walked into their assembly with fancy clothes and jewellery, the Hebrew Christians would rush to such a man or woman and say, "How nice to see you! You are most welcome here. Please take a seat down front." Then came along the tramp - the jobless, the poor man. Nobody rushed to meet him. "Oh no," they would say to themselves, "there's that man again. What are we going to do?" Finally in desperation they say, "You stand over there, please, or if you must sit, sit on the floor" (James 2:3, Phillips).

That is when James said, "You have despised the poor" (James 2:6). Then James asked, as it were, "By the way, has it worked?" The answer was no, it had not. "Do not rich men oppress you, and draw you before judgment seats?" (James 2:6). What folly those Hebrew Christians encountered! They thought that by catering to the rich they would win the rich. But it did not work. Not only did the wealthy non-Christians see right through these class-conscious Christians, they dragged them into court.

Apparently the Hebrew Christians thought they would get special favours from the wealthy by catering to them. It didn't work. What is more, they even gave those people a new vocabulary by which to blaspheme. "Do not they blaspheme that worthy name by the which ye are called?" (James 2:7).

It is here that I must interject what I believe is a relevant comment for evangelicalism today. When ever we are discriminate in our evangelism (wanting only a certain "type" - avoiding others) we bring judgment upon ourselves. I cannot exaggerate this. There is nothing that triggers God's anger more than our snobbishness and our neglect of the poor man. Christianity is the first enterprise in the history of the world that had something to offer the poor. "Go tell John this," said Jesus, "the blind receive their sight, and the lame walk, the lepers are cleansed, and the deaf hear, the dead are raised up, *and the poor have the gospel preached to them* (Matthew 11:4-5). This same James may have had some difference at first with the apostle Paul but they agreed on everything in the end "only they would that we should remember the poor; the same which I also was forward to do" (Galatians 2:10). When we aim for the rich we lose the poor man - and the rich man. Accept the poor and you will reach everybody. Everybody. Aim for the rich man and you will alienate him and incur God's judgment - I'm sure of it.

At this point James defends his position by the illustration of the Mosaic law. He quotes the command, "Thou shalt love thy neighbour as thyself" (James 2:8) which, according to Paul, fulfils the law "in one word" (Galatians 5:14). He shows them that if they are respecters of persons they "commit sin, and are convinced of the law as transgressors" (James 2:9). Those Hebrew Christians knew the law backwards and forwards but apparently had not realized that being a respecter of persons violated the law. "For whosoever shall keep the whole law, and yet offend in one point, he is guilty of all" (James 2:10). To prove that, James contrasts the seventh commandment with the sixth. "For he that said, Do not commit adultery, said also, Do not kill. Now if thou commit no adultery, yet if thou kill, thou art become a transgressor of the law" (James 2:11). At this juncture James inserts this application. "So speak ye, and so do, as they that shall be judged by the law of liberty" (James 2:12). After all, you have been set free, have you not? You have been given freedom from bondage. You therefore must extend this freedom to other people. But that is not all; for "judgment without mercy will be shown to anyone who has not been merciful" (James 2:13, NIV). It is precisely that very judgment that every Christian must fear who has shown contempt for the poor.

James is not speaking of a judgment that annuls one's salvation. The judgment he is speaking of is both the possibility of a sudden intervention of God in the present life and most certainty exposure at the judgment seat of Christ. James later says, "Go to now, ye rich men, weep and howl for your miseries that shalt come upon you" (James 5:1). The reason we know that one's salvation is not annulled is because James immediately says, "Mercy triumphs over judgment" (James 2:13). In other words, you have been saved unconditionally; you have been given freedom despite yourselves. That is precisely what the law of liberty is. If you, then, turn right around and withhold mercy from another when you have been given mercy, God will turn on you.

It is a great mistake to suppose that the Christian can escape the pain of God's displeasure - whether now or at the judgment seat of Christ. That is true with reference to any part of God's will in sanctification. As God promises to avenge sexual sin (1 Thessalonians 4:6), so also will He judge those who have neglected the poor. "He who is kind to the poor lends to the Lord, and he will reward him for what he has done" (Proverbs 19:17). James assured these oppressed believers that their cries "entered into the ears of the Lord of sabaoth" (James 5:4). For "judgment without mercy wilt be shown to anyone who has not been merciful (James 2:13).

Thus when James reaches 2:14 he is by no means finished with this discussion of the poor man. These Christians believed in justification by faith alone and in sound orthodoxy. But that is not the point, says James. "What doth it profit, my brethren, though a man say he hath faith, and have not works?" The "profit" is mainly with reference to what faith will do for other people. In the case of the poor man, what good is "faith"? "Can faith save him?" Can "faith" do anything for the poor man? Can faith "alone" save him? The *him is* not a reflexive pronoun; it is in the accusative singular just like *ptochon* in James 2:6.

But what to me makes the case all the more clear is, when you read the following verses with the aforementioned in mind you find, "If a brother or sister be naked, and destitute of daily food, and one of you say unto them, Depart in peace, be ye warmed and filled; *notwithstanding ye give them not those things which are needful to the body;* what doth it profit? (James 2:15-16). There is no doubt that the "profit" of James 2:16 refers to what will benefit the other person. One can see that this is precisely what James meant in 2:14. It is not a case of the person who has faith without works being saved or lost himself; it is what faith without works will do for another person: nothing. It is "dead, being alone" (James 2:17). The Greek word that is used in James 2:20 means "useless," which further shows what James meant in James 2:17. It does no good to say to another person, "God bless you" or "I believe in one God" (the devil believes that). The only thing that speaks to the other person - poor man or anybody else - is what is manifested in deeds.

Appendix 2

The writer of the epistle to the Hebrews addresses certain Christians who, despite a number of years in the Christian faith, were so "dull of hearing" that he was unable to say all he would have liked with reference to Melchizedek. He plainly puts the blame on them, "seeing ye are dull of hearing" (Hebrews 5:11). The writer feels that "by this time" they ought to be teachers but, alas, "you need someone to teach you the elementary truths of God's word all over again" (Hebrews 5:12, NIV).

This rebuke was more than a mere slap on the wrist. It was very grave indeed. The writer feared that these Christians might repeat what was so well known concerning the children of Israel who died in the wilderness (Hebrews 3:17). What he pleaded for, then, was a warm and docile heart in order that they might be sensitive to the voice of the Holy Spirit (Hebrews 3:7-12). But their being dull of hearing (slow to learn, NIV) gave the writer deep concern that these Hebrew Christians were ominously close to walking in the steps of their forefathers.

The writer begins Hebrews 6 with an exhortation to

"go on unto perfection," that is, full growth or maturity. Part of their problem had been that they thrived almost entirely on the ABCs, the elementary things - hearing the same old truths over and over again without it having the slightest effect on their spiritual aptitude to distinguish between good and evil (Hebrews 5:14). They were in danger of losing all sense of God's immediate voice to them, a sense of discernment to know the will of the Lord in the here and now.

Having listed six doctrines that we may gather to be what the writer means by ABCs (repentance, faith, baptisms, laying on of hands, resurrection of the dead, and eternal judgment), he expresses the hope that all will indeed go on to that perfection: "and this will we do, God permitting" (Hebrews 6:3).

There are two things that will bear our looking into by a closer examination of the original language.

1. The phrase "let us go on." This is expressed in the Greek rather unexpectedly in a passive form, which literally means "let us be carried on." It means to yield to a higher influence, as if the maturing process is not a matter of our own ingenuity, as one commentator puts it. In other words, the ability to go on is dependent upon the enabling grace of God. That is of crucial importance, as we shall see further below.

2. "This will we do, if God permit." This too is a phrase that may not seem so significant in the English translation. The force of the Greek suggests this translation: "God granting us mercy that we may be so enabled" (to go on to perfection). To put it another way, Hebrews 6:1 may go right into Hebrews 6:3 (with the aforementioned elementary doctrines placed in a paren-

thesis), thus reading: "Let us be carried on into perfection, and this we will do, God granting us mercy that we may be so enabled."

Why this explanation? Because of the word *for* in Hebrews 6:4. The reason the writer says *for* is because of his knowledge of the children of Israel in the Old Testament and, more particularly, his knowledge of certain persons that had been a part of that very Christian community. For the description that follows (six graces: repentance, illumination, tasting the heavenly gift, being made partakers of the Holy Spirit, tasting the good Word of God, and tasting the powers of the age to come) is enough to show that wonderful achievements in things spiritual provide no guarantee that one will (1) enter into God's rest and (2) not fall away, thus missing what might be one's own inheritance. In other words, when the writer knows full well what has happened to some, he is compelled to say, "This will we do, God granting us mercy that we may be so enabled." For - or because - we know about others, don't we? That is why he begins Hebrews 6:4 with *for*.

Concerning Hebrews 6:4-6, I have come across eight different positions. There is the Arminian position: those described in Hebrews 6:4-6 were truly converted but the falling away means they lost their salvation. As I have said, the Arminians (not surprisingly) never make too much of this passage because none of them (that I have met) really believe it: they are always pleading with those who have fallen away to be "reclaimed" or "restored."

There are four Calvinist positions that I know of (1) Those described in Hebrews 6:4-6 are truly converted but the *if* proves that it is hypothetical. It could never happen in actual fact. (2) Those described in Hebrews 6:4-6 are saved, but the falling away is not with reference to loss of salvation but inability to be renewed again unto repentance. In other words, it means exactly what it says. (3) Those described in Hebrews 6:4-6 have a non-working work of grace in them. What happened to them was real, but it was not saving; they were never converted in the first place. (4) Those described in Hebrews 6:4-6 are truly converted people, but if it should turn out that they fall away, one must but conclude they were not saved after all.

There are three "neutral" positions, although those presumably might uphold the teaching of "once saved, always saved." (1) The writer is only showing that the foundation cannot be laid a second time; that there is no such thing as a second repentance. (2) The failure to repent is true *while* they are crucifying Christ afresh; it is impossible to be renewed *as long* as they are in a state of falling away. (3) The "impossibility" refers to the outlook from man's point of view, not God's point of view. In other words, from God's point of view it is always possible.

Those are the eight positions that I have come across. No doubt there are others, if not also variations on those I have described. My own position, having looked long and hard at all the options I know of, is that Hebrews 6:4-6 describes saved people who could not be renewed again unto repentance

When the writer begins this section with *for,* he is primarily showing us that having repented, having been illuminated, and so on is no *guarantee* that one will (1)

enter into God's rest (maturity) and (2) not fall away so that it will be impossible to be renewed again unto repentance. The six descriptions indicate not only a valid conversion but considerable progress as well. Yet such progress does not in and of itself guarantee that all will enter into rest - "For ..." It is as though he says, "For we know all too well, don't we, about those who did repent and were illuminated and made partakers of the Holy Spirit and fell away."

Let us look at the word *impossible*. The first thing we must do is to see how else the word is used by our writer. Whereas in Hebrews 6:4-6 it is a reference to the impossibility of renewal again unto repentance, in Hebrews 6:18 it refers to the impossibility for God to lie. In Hebrews 10:4 it refers to the impossibility of the blood of animals to remove sin. In Hebrews 11:6 it refers to the impossibility of pleasing God without faith. We must conclude therefore that the word *impossible* cannot be diluted, however much we may wish to try.

But what is the object of what is impossible? A renewal again unto repentance. That proves there had been repentance in the first place. Surely that is enough to show that the people described were converted. If those people had repented, they were converted. The writer says they could not be renewed again unto repentance; that shows there was repentance in the first place. The word used is *metanoia* It means "change of mind." It means "agreeing with God" or saying "I was wrong."

There must be a renewal of repentance in the Christian life if there is to be a hearing of the voice of the Holy Spirit. The warm and docile heart that the writer is after is attained to only by continual repentance. What worried the writer was that those Christians had already become "dull of hearing." We know that at the natural level there are those who begin to lose their hearing. It must be a most melancholy experience. I pray it will never happen to me. How lovely to hear my wife's voice, my children speaking to me, the singing of birds, the sound of music. But there is something worse than that. It is to become hard of hearing - spiritually. To no longer feel smitten for sin, feel convicted about this or that, sense the will of God in a crisis, know what the Spirit is saying to us - that is the loss of hearing that is most serious of all.

The writer warns that it is possible for a Christian to lose this sensitivity to the Spirit's voice. If there is not a constant "walking in the light" (1 John 1:7), one is in a precarious position; one is in danger of becoming hard of hearing at the spiritual level. In a word: that to which those people could not be renewed was the inward capacity to grasp God's call to them - the clear mind, objectivity of things, lucidity.

This interpretation of Hebrews 6:4-6 is carried out without the slightest manipulation. It seems to me that the other attempts to explain this passage border on superimposing a preconceived entrenched position on these verses. I myself have had to change my view. It has given me great peace, and my new position has stood up to some of the severest questioning one can imagine.

I think it would be of interest to know something of the ancient history of interpretation of this passage. It is not a happy story, but here are the facts. Justin Martyr called "illumination" baptism. By his doing that the word spread throughout the Christian community in the second century that anybody who fell away after baptism would be eternally lost. It is incredible that many believed that but they did. For one thing (which is the saddest of all), there was an astonishing lack of understanding of the grace of God in the second and third centuries. The apostolic fathers were good, moral men - many of whom were willing to die for Christ. But many of them were theologically barren, insofar as understanding grace is concerned. It is not until you read men like Athanasius and Augustine that there may be seen a robust understanding of the grace of God. The state of Christianity became so bleak in some places that the Christian faith degenerated into sheer morality.

A proof of that is a second-century work called *The Shepherd* written by Hermas. This document reflects a widespread consternation among many Christians at the time who feared they were eternally doomed to perdition because they had sinned since their baptism. Hermas wrote *The Shepherd* partly to say that God had revealed to him that there is forgiveness of sins at least once after baptism This book was reportedly responsible for encouraging a vast number of Christians. But there was one famous man who was taking no chances. His name was Constantine. Although he professed to have become a Christian, he delayed his own baptism for many years because he did not want to risk sinning after baptism.

The writer of Hebrews did not have such problems in mind, nor did he have a deficient theology of the grace of God. He was warning believers of the danger of professing to be saved but living like the world. When one professes faith in Jesus Christ, it is because repen-

225

tance has come into the picture. But there have been those who, having repented of their sins and trusted Jesus Christ alone for salvation, fell into sin. Some of such people came out of it, as did the man described by Paul in 1 Corinthians 5. It would also seem that those very people described in Hebrews 6:4-6 had been formerly renewed to repentance; otherwise the writer makes no sense when he says renewed "again" (Gr. *palin*). It would appear then that two things lay behind this passage: (1) the writer knew the very people he described; (2) those people had been through the renewal process before. But they reached the place where nobody could help them. They became stone deaf.

I should like to make a few more observations. If people who have repented, been illuminated and made partakers of the Holy Spirit, are not saved, when will they ever know that they are? It is argued by some that those people were never converted. If that is true, when would such people ever believe that they were converted? For example, if I am told that I could be illuminated, having repented of my sins, and even been made a partaker of the Holy Spirit, but that I could still be "dead in trespasses and sins," what will it take for me to believe I have moved beyond these descriptions of Hebrews 6:4-6 What on earth will it take to convince me I am not in that class? If I find that these verses describe me - repentance, illumination, partaking of the Spirit, and so on - am I to believe I am not saved?

Those Hebrew Christians were already discouraged. Hebrews 10:35 is proof of that. Am I to believe that the writer would be so pastorally insensitive as to come along and describe such lofty graces and then say, "But these people were never saved"? Who could ever exceed such descriptions (which, presumably, would be necessary to be sure one is truly converted)? Surely the very signs that people would want if they needed evidences of conversion are precisely these. In other words, if they were to look for signs they would look for those six descriptions. It seems to me that to conclude those people were never saved in the first place comes awfully close to demoralising any Christian. I do not think that is the spirit of the New Testament.

Furthermore, pastoral experience has shown that hundreds of thousands of people who have fallen have realized their own folly and come out of it. Jonah fell. He was given a second chance. David fell. He was granted repentance.

The writer of Hebrews knew these people. They apparently had been through the cycle of renewal unto repentance before. But it would seem that they reached the place that they could not be renewed "again." They were beyond help. Those our Lord addressed in Ephesus had fallen but they apparently were not beyond help: "Remember therefore from whence thou art fallen, and repent, and do the first works" (Revelation 2:5). Those Paul addresses in Galatians had fallen but apparently they were not beyond help: "I travail in birth again until Christ be formed in you" (Galatians 4:19).

The people the writer of Hebrews addresses had somehow put the name of Christ into such disrepute that it was the same as crucifying Christ "afresh" (Gr. *anastaurountas* - re-crucifying). It is as though such careless living put Christ back on the cross again, for their lives brought His name into "open shame." It may

227

have been something as disgraceful as the situation of Corinth (1 Corinthians 5); I don't know. But it seems obvious to me that the writer had good reason for making the statement about them that he did. And yet the man in 1 Corinthians 5 was a converted man.

Hebrews 6:7-8 are analogous to John 15 and 1 Corinthians 3. Some have thought that the parable of the sower (Matthew 13:3-23) should be set alongside Hebrews 6:7-8. I too thought this once, but a careful analysis will not hold up a connection between the parable of the sower and Hebrews 6:7-8, if only because there is no indication that those who "fell by the way-side," or "on stony ground," or "among thorns" were never allowed an opportunity for a better kind of growth. Moreover, in the parable of the sower it was a case of seed falling "among thorns"; in Hebrews 6:8 the land "produced thorns," that is, the opposite of fruit. So what does one do with thorns and briers? One burns them. Why? They are useless. That is what the writer says: "whose end is to be burned" (Hebrews 6:8). It is exactly the same thing Jesus said about the vine that does not bear fruit in John 15:6. The burning in Hebrews 6:8, then, is analogous to the "saved so as by fire" in 1 Corinthians 3:15.

Index
of Names and Subjects

Index of Scripture